Reading Nasta'liq

Bibliotheca Iranica consists of:
Persian Fiction in Translation Series
Performing Arts Series
Literature Series
Reprint Series
Special Persian Language Publication Series

Bibliotheca Iranica
Literature Series No. 3

Reading Nasta'liq

Persian and Urdu Hands From 1500 to the Present

by
William L. Hanaway
and
Brian Spooner

MAZDA PUBLISHERS ❧ Costa Mesa, California ❧ 1995

Mazda Publishers
Since 1980
P.O. Box 2603
Costa Mesa, California 92626 U.S.A.

Library of Congress Cataloging-in-Publication Data

Reading Nasta`liq: Persian and Urdu Hands from 1500 to the Present/
[Complied by] William L. Hanaway and Brian Spooner.
p. cm.—(Bibliotheca Iranica. Literature Series; No. 3)
Includes bibliographical references.
ISBN:1-56859-033-4 (alk. paper)
1. Persian language—Writing. 2. Urdu language—Writing.
I. Hanaway, William L., 1929-. II. Spooner, Brian.
PK6228.K43 1995
491'.5511—dc20
94-35249
CIP

1 3 5 7 9 10 8 6 4 2

انتشارات مزدا

If learning in general has met with such little encouragement, still less can be expected for that branch of it which lies so far removed from the common path, and which the greater part of mankind have hitherto considered as incapable of yielding either entertainment or instruction: if pains and want be the lot of a scholar, the life of an orientalist must certainly be attended with peculiar hardships (Jones 1771, p. ix).

We dedicate this book
to present and future Orientalists
to help ease some of the "peculiar hardships."

CONTENTS

PREFACE

When we reflect on the difficulties that frequently occur among ourselves, in reading the familiar letters of our friends: when we consider that many are puzzled in deciphering even what has been written by themselves, we cannot wonder that more serious obstacles are presented to the learner of a new language, and a strange character: a character, too, that, from its construction, and the facility with which combinations may be formed, allows the writer to indulge in infinite liberties (Ouseley 1795, p. viii).

The project that has resulted in this book first took on objective form in July, 1990, when we convened a workshop on handwriting in the context of Penn's Persian language program. The design of that workshop reflected our general orientation towards the place of Persian studies in the larger curriculum.

Persian differs from most other languages with which it is commonly compared by virtue of a number of factors that have been neglected in recent decades. Firstly, Persian has been taught in Western universities longer than most other non-European languages (though it is currently taught in relatively few institutions). Secondly, although it is now best known as the national language of a single country, Iran, under other names it is also the national language of Tajikistan and the official language of Afghanistan, and it is widely spoken in Uzbekistan, Pakistan, and the Persian Gulf area. Thirdly, due to the fact that it had served as the koine of the eastern, non-Arabic-speaking Islamic world until the nineteenth century, Persian continues to play the role of classical language, similar to Latin in the West, from as far east as the towns around the Takla Makan in Xinjiang to Sarajevo in the west.

The major factors in the spread and durability of Persian beyond the communities of native speakers (who were historically only a minority of the total number of users) were literary and bureaucratic. Most people spoke either local dialects or other Iranian languages in much of Iran, Afghanistan, and Tajikistan; or one or another form of Turkic throughout the area, including the Balkans, Anatolia, and Central and Inner Asia; or one or another Indo-Aryan or Dravidian language in South Asia. The current dominance of Persian as a spoken language in Iran, Tajikistan, and most of Afghanistan is a product of modern education and literacy.

As a result, literacy in Persian today is not the simple equivalent of literacy in most other cultural traditions, even those such as Arabic that have a long literary tradition supported by religious considerations. The study of Persian handwriting similarly has a particular significance. However, this is a study that has been chronically neglected and poorly supported by any type of teaching aid.

In the workshop we attempted to take account of this special character of Persian literacy. We also included Urdu because of the close historical relationship between the literary and bureaucratic usage, and the script, of the two languages. We are grateful to Iraj Anvar, Latifeh Hagigi, Ahmad Karimi-Hakkak, Wilma Heston, Manuchehr Kashef, Hamid Mahamadi, Ahmad Mahdavi-Damghani, Mehdi Marashi, Senzil Nawid, John Perry, Zhaleh Pirnazar, Frances Pritchett, and Kazem Tehrani, who attended. Although the workshop produced no immediate result, the enthusiasm of the participants and the ideas and materials that they contributed ensured that our interest remained active, and we are conscious of how much we learned from the discussions that they generated.

Clarification of our objectives over the following years led us to convene a more specialized workshop in June 1993. This was attended by Michael Beard, Walter Feldman, Peter Gaeffke, Wilma Heston, Ahmad Mahdavi-Damghani, C.M. Naim, Senzil Nawid, John Perry, and Frances Pritchett. We are especially grateful to them for focusing their attention with us on the subject matter of this book. Since then we have worked closely with C.M. Naim and Frances Pritchett, who contributed the Urdu passages; with Bruce Pray who provided some of the Persian material and commented in detail on the Urdu; with Ahmad Mahdavi-Damghani, John Perry, and Hushang Rahnama, who read and commented in detail on the Persian; with Shamsur Rahman Faruqi who did the same for both the Persian and the Urdu. Special thanks go also to John Emerson, Lorraine Hanaway, Wilma Heston, and Ezat O. Negahban for special help when it was most needed. All have been unstinting with their time and have given us invaluable assistance. Frederick Schoch took exceptional care in photographing the examples, which were of uneven quality. Finally, we are especially grateful to Ahmad Mahdavi-Damghani not only for responding patiently in this as in other projects to our endless questions, but also for writing out the examples in the Guide.

We also take this opportunity to express our gratitude to the International Center of the U.S. Department of Education for financial assistance for the workshops (under the Title VI Program), and to the University of Pennsylvania's Research Foundation for funds toward manuscript preparation and publication.

We have striven to give the most accurate readings possible, but in many cases the writing is ambiguous or illegible. Where we could see no alternative we have put down what seems to be required, but in some cases we have indicated our doubts. While we are fully aware how much we are indebted to everyone who has helped us with the many problems of producing a book like this, we are sensible (in Sir William Jones' words) "that it falls very short of perfection, which seems to withdraw itself from the pursuit of mortals, in proportion to their endeavours of attaining it."

William L. Hanaway and Brian Spooner
University of Pennsylvania, June 20, 1995

INTRODUCTION

This book deals with handwriting in the Perso-Arabic script, a subject that has received relatively little attention, especially in recent decades. It was conceived as an aid to research in historical and other textual materials written in the styles known as *nasta'liq* and *shekasta*. It assumes a knowledge of either Persian or Urdu, and is intended as an aid only to reading, not to writing. It contains no translations or explicit interpretations, but focuses exclusively on the analysis and decipherment of handwritten script, that is, on one formal dimension of the textual record. The subject matter overlaps with the fields of palaeography and diplomatics. The book is likely to be most useful to advanced students and to scholars engaged in independent documentary research, whether in the humanities or the social sciences. But it will also be useful to anyone who needs to read any type of handwriting in Persian or Urdu, and perhaps also in some other historically related languages.

Much has changed in the fields of Persian and Urdu studies in the past generation, particularly in the United States. Although they have diverged and now relatively few scholars learn both languages, neither field has been caught up in the modernization programs that have affected instruction in other modern languages. In the Persian field, recruitment, disciplinary balance, and the image of the field itself have been transformed by the effects of the political changes in Iran. Neither field fits easily in the current classification of academia or the liberal arts curriculum. The reasons that underlay earlier scholarly interest in Persian and Urdu now are largely forgotten or misunderstood. They include the unique nature of the relationship in Persian (and to some extent also in Urdu) between the spoken and the written language, which is different not only from other languages in the curriculum, but also from the type of diglossia that is common in other Asian and Middle Eastern languages such as Arabic, Hindi or Chinese. In both fields, however, the actual writing has always been underrepresented in formal instruction. One consequence of recent changes both in these fields and in the larger academic environment is further neglect of this formal dimension.

Both Persian and Urdu have a rich literary and bureaucratic heritage that is carried in their respective written traditions. Written Persian was both uniform and international, read in the past over a vast area of Asia. The spoken language, in contrast, is current today in a much smaller area, and though to some extent standardized by modern education, it varies significantly by locality and social class. Although neither language is immune to the processes that have affected most major languages in modern times, their literary and bureaucratic heritage more than balances the dynamics of modern speech as the languages evolve today.

This balance has important implications for programs of instruction, but in modern language programs in the United States it is difficult to maintain. Until recently, most teachers of Persian were non-native speakers, primarily interested in textual research. Typically they had little or no ambition to attain high levels of proficiency in the spoken language, but they showed great sensitivity to the difficulties of non-native speakers attempting to develop competence in the written language. Nevertheless, when students (including the authors of this book) set out to conduct research using manuscript materials, they invariably faced considerable frustration with the difficulty of the script. Recent efforts to reorient language instruction to give greater attention to the spoken form. of the language have exacerbated the situation. Where attention is now given to the written word it is given almost exclusively to the printed form of the language, to the *naskh* style of the script, or to the nasta‘liq style written according to calligraphic standards. The student or scholar who finds it necessary to read an Iranian colleague's ordinary everyday handwriting, to say nothing of an office memorandum written for a professional colleague a century or so ago, is reduced to the social (and academic) status of an illiterate.

The opening quotation shows that early Western students of Persian were not only aware of the nature of the problem, but they had also defined some of its dimensions. For example, elsewhere Ouseley wrote:

> So confused, inaccurate, and uncouth is the shekasteh hand, and so much has it degenerated from the parent nishkhi, that many even among the natives of Hindoostan ... are puzzled for hours in striving to decipher particular words, and, after all, are probably indebted to the context for their success in ascertaining the sense (ibid. pp. 4-5).

Context is important for reading handwriting in any language. For the non-native reader, however, making the transition from one's own script to the Perso-Arabic script is not straightforward. For various reasons, having to do with differences in the tools and the position of writing (see the description in Faza'eli 2536, pp. 55-112) and the direction and mechanics of the script, we can happily concur with H. D. G. Law who wrote:

> The deciphering of Persian manuscripts is an exercise with a distinct entertainment value ... (1948, p. 5). As in the case with the deciphering of a difficult handwriting in any language, even the reader's own, a certain 'flair,' which really cannot be taught, is necessary; a facility for making the inspired guess. Apart from that, the main essential is a sound knowledge of the language; for without that one cannot even make an intelligent guess; and to this, of course, there is no short cut (ibid., p. 7).

We agree that besides an understanding of the context "a certain 'flair'" is invaluable. But even flair benefits greatly from experience. Developing it on one's own can be a long and arduous, even forbidding task. And neither context nor flair are entirely reliable aids: they can lead the reader to read what is not there. We hope that the analysis of selected passages which is presented below will shorten the time needed for the scholar to develop the reading skills that are essential for serious research.

I

Most Persian documents since about 1500 have been written in styles of script known as nasta‘liq and shekasta. Nasta‘liq derives from a combination of two earlier styles of script, namely, naskh and *ta‘liq*, and has also been referred to as *naskh-e ta‘liq*, and *naskhta‘liq*. It began to be recognized as an independent form in the second half of the fourteenth century (Faza’eli 1391, pp. 444-45). Early nasta‘liq existed in a western style and an eastern style. The former, practiced at the court of Sultan Ya‘qub Aq Qoyunlu, relatively soon fell out of favor, but traces of it are said to survive in the nasta‘liq of Afghanistan and the Subcontinent. The eastern style, developed in Khorasan, rapidly gained general acceptance and one authority estimates that by the middle of the fifteenth century, three-fourths of everything written in Iran was in nasta‘liq (ibid., pp. 448-50). The use of nasta‘liq soon spread to the Ottoman Empire where it was used for writing both Turkish and Persian, while in the Subcontinent it was adopted as the normative vehicle for writing Urdu. It has also influenced writing styles in Egypt and some other Arabic-speaking lands, where it has sometimes been called *farsi*. With the spread of nasta‘liq, the use of ta‘liq for writing Persian rapidly declined (ibid., p. 601).

As ta‘liq became more widely used for writing Persian in the fourteenth century, writers using it for bureaucratic and other non-calligraphic purposes, especially in administration and commerce, found it convenient to streamline the script so that it could be written more quickly and easily. As a result, a "broken" (shekasta) form evolved in which some letters were greatly reduced in size, while others were written with thinner strokes or given new shapes; most significantly, letters that in the formal versions of the Arabic script cannot connect to the left were made to connect. This *shekasta-ye ta‘liq*, as it was called, became very popular for everyday purposes and was even used by calligraphers (ibid., p. 405).

When nasta‘liq began to supplant ta‘liq at the end of the fifteenth century it was affected by the same evolutionary process. In its early form, as it was used, for example, in the court of Shah ‘Abbas II, the "broken" form of nasta‘liq was called *shafi‘a’i* and *shafi‘a* (ibid., pp. 613-14, 639), but by the late sixteenth century it was called *shekasta-ye nasta‘liq*, and eventually simply shekasta. Since early writers of it had been trained in shekasta-ye ta‘liq, there are clear ta‘liq influences in some of its forms (ibid., pp. 407-8). In the seventeenth century shekasta-ye nasta‘liq rapidly replaced shekasta-ye ta‘liq as well as other styles for everyday professional use.

By the nineteenth century some felt that the process of streamlining had advanced too far. Much shekasta writing had become unduly complicated and difficult to read. Consequently, efforts were made to simplify it. The result was a broad array of nasta‘liq styles containing elements of shekasta that made up a composite style known as *shekasta-amiz*. This style became predominant in the areas where nasta'liq was the preferred calligraphic style, namely, the non-Arabic-speaking parts of the Ottoman Empire, the Caucasus, Iran, Afghanistan, Central Asia (including western Xinjiang), and in the Subcontinent under the Moghul empire. In India it was also used for Urdu, and in the West it was applied for some literary and diplomatic purposes to Ottoman Turkish. It has also been used for some other Turkic languages.

Nasta'liq and shekasta styles continued to evolve, and shekasta-amiz continues in common use today. However, in this century the tradition was broken over the northern part of the area: in the Caucasus, Transcaucasia and Transcaspia by Sovietization starting in 1922, and in Turkey by Romanization in 1928. The tradition also lapsed in China after 1949. Since the 1980s there have been moves to revive shekasta-amiz in some of the ex-Soviet parts of the area, and with the reemergence of independent states such moves have enjoyed some official encouragement, especially in Tajikistan. Nasta'liq has also been the vehicle for the spread of literacy among speakers of certain South Asian languages such as Kashmiri, but has not been used in others whose literary traditions began independently of Urdu, such as Pashto and Sindhi. Today nasta'liq remains the model for teaching handwriting in Persian and Urdu in the region and naskh has become the standard form for Persian printing. Urdu printing has remained predominantly nasta'liq.

We are faced with the anomaly that although documents in nasta'liq and shekasta represent the most important archive of materials for research in the late medieval and modern history and literature of most of central and western Asia and the Subcontinent, most Persian and Urdu language courses in the West pay little or no attention to it. The few published works that are available as aids to the study of the script (see the Annotated Bibliography at the end of this volume) are interesting more for historical than practical purposes. Students are taught to read only the printed text, which is naskh. To some extent they may be taught to decipher calligraphic nasta'liq to enable them to read poetry, which is sometimes published in calligraphy. In the past students typically were taught formal grammar and texts, and were left to pick up everyday speech and handwriting on their own. The new emphasis on native speech has had the effect of further reducing attention to reading and writing. Whether or not our educational objectives should be performance at the level of native speakers, or even native writers, is open to debate. To be able to speak like a non-native speaker but read like a native reader is, perhaps, within easier reach and more necessary for usual academic purposes. Such, anyway, is the rationale for this publication.

Even though the place of handwriting is changing in Iran, as in most of the world, Persians still read their own handwriting with ease and fluency, even if they often encounter the same problems in deciphering "illegible" hands as we do in English. Culture in Iran is still carried through the handwritten word much more than is the case in the West. Second-script acquisition is not entirely comparable with second-language acquisition. It may be easy at the elementary levels, but at more advanced levels it involves training the eye independently of purely linguistic knowledge. At the same time, understanding how native readers read can help in the interpretation of what they write. For example, Baluch in Iran who go through the educational system, or otherwise become literate, are educated in Persian and read and write Persian, which is their second or third language at best. When confronted with publications in their own language, Baluchi, they typically have great difficulty reading it, although the script is identical with the Persian script. This suggests that Persians, although their script is largely phonetic, more so certainly than English, do not read in the simple alphabetic-phonetic way that we generally think we do, but rather ideographically in words, penstrokes, or even larger patterns, to a somewhat greater extent than we do.

In Urdu the handwritten script occupies a much more prominent position than it does in Persian because practically all printed Urdu is actually reproduced from copy handwritten by professional scribes. But Urdu is no better served with materials for acquiring native reader capability than is Persian. For a long time many of the people who wrote Urdu also wrote Persian. The habit of writing two languages has the same consequences as bilingualism, especially as it relates to convergence between the two textual traditions. We consider that there is much to learn about the writing of each language from the study of the other. The divorce between Persian and Urdu scholarship that has occurred since the middle of the century makes it more difficult to see many of the factors that would increase our understanding and appreciation of each.

II

It remains to give a brief account of the principles underlying the selection and order of the following Examples, and how they are intended to be used. The Examples are grouped in six sections. The first five are Persian, and follow each other in roughly chronological order. The sixth section is Urdu. Within each section the Examples are ordered, very broadly, according to impressions of increasing difficulty. After spending considerable effort and time experimenting with different arrangements, we have decided that there is no single ordering of the Examples that would satisfy the criterion of a rationalized system. We have, therefore, settled on sequences that, while necessarily impressionistic in detail, still represent a general progression from easy to difficult. Since practice and a wide exposure to different hands are crucial in learning to read nasta‘liq and shekasta, elaborate schemes based on elusive criteria seemed likely to be less useful to the student than this compromise. At the beginning of each section is a brief description of its contents.

While no selection of this size can be fully representative of such a vast archive, we have attempted to include a broad range of types of official and non-official hands and of features that are rarely described in the literature. The sources themselves are indicated after each passage and described briefly in the Bibliography.

Different readers are likely to want to use this book in different ways, depending on their interests and their prior experience with the script. However, the following suggestions may be useful. Although the obvious way to proceed is probably to start at the beginning and apply each transcription to its original, letter by letter, such an approach may be the least productive. Large parts of these Examples, if approached in this way, may deceptively appear to be quite straightforward, and such readers will deprive themselves of the unique learning experience that we ourselves have undergone over the past year as we have worked towards this final text. For the general reader, the most productive approach, and one that we recommend strongly, is the opposite: select any Example that looks relatively easy, in which you can make out many words, and try to read it completely down to the last detail, without assuming anything. Do not give up until you have systematically tried all the possibilities you can think of for decipherment, in most cases a matter of hours at least. When you wind up with a definite number of difficulties, look at the notes and then at the Guide that follows this introduction. Where they do not help you, remember that the notes are cumulative. Go back to Ex. 1, and attempt the same exercise. Then work forward to where you started.

Some features are peculiar to subsections and may seem of little interest to readers specializing in other periods or types of documents. It should be remembered, however, that although the use of the script was widespread, the number of individuals using it before the middle of this century was not very large. It is not an exaggeration to speak of a nasta'liq community. Although there are individual styles and idiosyncrasies, anything that occurred in one place in the tradition provides clues that may assist the reader somewhere else in the same tradition.

In their informal, rapidly-written varieties, whether from the hands of bureaucrats or professional scribes before modern education, or from the growing percentage of literate citizens today, materials in these scripts present serious obstacles to historians and literary scholars in their use of primary sources. We made a point of selecting examples which on the one hand are ordinary everyday handwriting for particular times, places or social situations, but on the other are likely to be relatively difficult for non-native readers (in some cases also for experienced native readers). We have largely avoided long documents, so that each Example could be complete. In four cases it was necessary to reduce the size of the original document to allow it to fit on the page, and in each case this has been mentioned in the Notes.

The overall intent is practical: to provide systematic support for graduate training in reading the nasta'liq and shekasta styles of the Perso-Arabic script, including both medieval manuscripts and modern handwriting. Much of the material in our Examples is, by nature, difficult to read in any language and presents special problems in Persian and Urdu. Although this book is to a large extent historically organized, it is in no measure a history of writing styles. It is, rather, a practical manual that can be used both by instructors as class material and by students working independently. It is not representative of Persian writing generally. It does not provide models for learning to write, and it should not be understood to imply any criteria for evaluating different hands or features. Our approach is purely empirical and analytical, with the aim of helping students to see the analytical dimensions of reading as a skill, independent of linguistic knowledge but essential to a comprehensive understanding of a literate tradition, especially one as rich as Persian and Urdu. Apart from opening up a neglected dimension of language study, we hope it will facilitate and promote research in primary sources.

Note on Romanization

We have designed this book for use by readers who know Persian and/or Urdu, and for this reason we have simplified the romanization of Persian and Urdu words by omitting diacritical marks. For romanizing Persian consonants we have used the IJMES system without diacritics. Persian vowels are rendered as *a, e, o, a, i, u,* and the diphthongs as *ow, ey*. The final silent *h* is represented by *a*. For Urdu, we have used the Library of Congress system without diacritics.

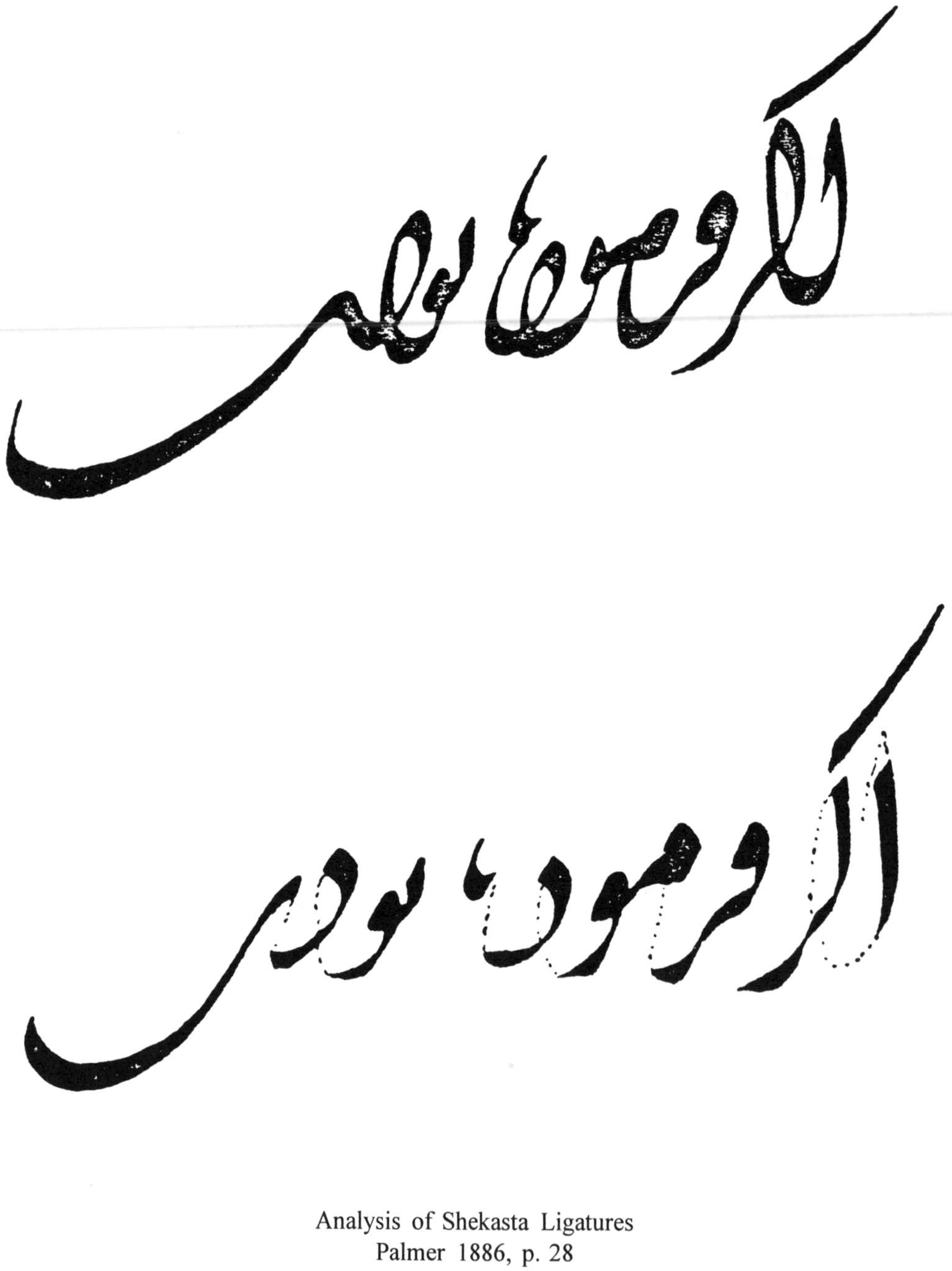

Analysis of Shekasta Ligatures
Palmer 1886, p. 28

GUIDE TO COMMON FEATURES OF SHEKASTA

After each Example of nasta'liq and shekasta in this book we have provided annotations, commenting on points of interest and suggesting explanations where the transcription itself may not suffice to enable the reader to reconstruct how a particular deformation arose out of the underlying standard form. Many of these points deserve discussion on a more general level, and we introduce them here in order to facilitate comparison and contrast, and at the same time to develop the necessary terminology for discussion. The points are numbered sequentially throughout for ease of reference. In references below to the Examples the number after the colon indicates the line number. Names of letters are italicized. Persian words in transliteration, as well as English words introduced as descriptive terms, are italicized on the first occurrence.

I. General Considerations

(1) In working from the general to the particular, we begin with considerations that encroach on the subject matter of diplomatics, but which are equally important for the more restricted objectives of this volume: the range of conventions relating to the organization of the text on a page. Where Western texts are broken up by paragraphing, punctuation, and other familiar formatting strategies, in the Perso-Arabic script similar effects are achieved by other means. A Persian or Urdu writer may begin at the same level down the page as a writer of English. But he is unlikely to indent. The beginning of the text of a formal document, after any preliminary material such as a salutation, was often indicated by a long overlining across the extent of the text. This practice may have originated in the extension of the medial ligature of *al-'abd*, or *ba'd*, and one or other of these words does in fact appear clearly in some examples (see Exx. 11 and 12) in ways directly comparable to what appears to be simple overlining in others (such as Exx. 10 and 13). The writer first draws the line across the page, and then starts to write just beneath it. He is not disturbed when some of the letters rise through it, which commonly happens because of the tendency to *stack* words at the end of the line. Overlining may therefore give the inexperienced reader the erroneous impression that the initial line of text is crossed out (cf. Ex. 16).

(2) Short overlinings also serve as an important form of punctuation, to draw attention, similar to the way underlining can be used in the Latin script. The difference derives from the different orientation to the line, from the fact that the Perso-Arabic script is written not on the line, but along it. Short overlinings are used to signal a change of

topic, equivalent to a new paragraph (cf. especially Ex. 4, but it is common throughout), and to signal the beginning of a new poem, as in Ex. 69:6. The short horizontal line may begin with an initial hook, and has been explained as originating from the second penstroke of the word *babat*. Proper names may be marked in the same way.

(3) Underlining is also used, but apparently only for numbers. It is discussed below in no. 12.

(4) One other symbol of this type which deserves mention resembles a shekasta form of extended *re* run into final *he* (cf. below no. 71), and signals a line of poetry (*bayt*) inserted in the text. It appears in Ex. 70:5.

(5) Within the text a new chapter may be announced by larger or bolder letters (comparable to mediaeval European mss.): see Ex. 4:8.

(6) The distance between lines tends to diminish from the top to the bottom of the page. Lines become closer and shorter towards the bottom of the page, and sometimes the writing also diminishes in size. The *Dastur-e Dabiri* (see Bibliography) relates this to the standing (*qadr*) of the writer: the greater the writer, the greater the distance is left between the lines, and vice-versa (p. 13).

(7) The *Dastur-e Dabiri* (p. 28) says that in the interior of a letter the writer should write across the entire width of the paper, evenly. If he leaves any space on the right, he should be careful to keep the beginnings of the lines straight so that it would be obvious if anything were added to the beginning of any of them. It is the practice of accountants to leave space at the end of each line in case a calculation should become necessary in the course of the letter, but once again the margin should be kept straight (ibid.). When the writer reaches the bottom of the page, instead of turning over or moving to the next sheet, he is more likely to turn to the margins (if he has left any). He will turn the page around and write on the slant from the bottom right hand margin back up to the top of the page, continue along the top and down the left hand margin, turning the page as he goes. Example 34 illustrates this well, as do several others. Ex. 4 shows the margins being used in a lithographed text in a way more familiar to readers of European mss.

(8) The text often ends either with a formulaic *faqat* (which may be reduced to a logograph), or a conventional "[the writer] gives no more trouble," which may also be reduced to little more than a single penstroke (cf. Exx. 6, 7, 8, 9, 12, 15, 18, 30, 36, 37, 44, 47, 50, 72).

(9) Finally, a signature at the end of a document may be couched in or supported by the extended internal ligature of the words *al-'abd* again. In some cases the signature appears to have been written on the envelope rather than at the bottom of the text.

(10) Many examples from various periods end with an almost identical flourish (see Exx. 30, 34, 35, 36, 39, 41, 44, 47, 48, 51, 61, 62), the significance of which is unclear but which could be, in effect, "nothing follows."

(11) Other conventions relating to the organization of space on the page include, for example, writing the legal opinion on the top left (with the page turned through 90 degrees to the left), while the plaintiff acknowledges it on the top right (with the page turned through 90 degrees to the right; see for example the instance in Exx. 11 and 13).

(12) In dates the *sin* of *sana* (year) is typically extended to form a bed for the number of the year, which is given as a numeral. The ligature in the suffix (*-om*) of ordinal numerals is similarly extended as a bed for the number of the day of the month. Numerals may also be embedded in an extended shekasta form of *nomra*. Other numerals are generally marked by a line drawn underneath, perhaps derived from this embedding, where there is no convenient ligature to support them. The number of the day of the month is typically followed by a mark resembling an exaggerated comma, starting at mid-line and extending at about seven o'clock to a point below the imaginary line along which the number is written. According to the *Dastur-e Dabiri*, "whatever is written by those in power must have a date .... Whatever the *divan* of the powerful writes, the date should be at the end, and whatever is from lesser individuals, the date should be at the beginning, after the *sadr* ..." (pp. 21-22).

(13) Most of the conventions of shekasta derive from calligraphic nasta‘liq (or, in some cases, ta‘liq). Partly for this reason we chose to begin both the Persian and the Urdu sections of the book with calligraphic examples. The reader may find it helpful also to review a manual of calligraphy, such as the work of Faza'eli which is listed in the bibliography. In calligraphy the major concern is not speed but the need to accommodate all the penstrokes that make up each line (or, in the case of poetry, half line) to the aesthetic requirements of the organization of space on the page.

(14) Various conventions are therefore traceable to such forces as the need to *cram* in more penstrokes than could be accommodated in a straight line, which is often achieved by *stacking* at the end of the line (see, e.g., Ex. 36). In non-calligraphic contexts this can lead to considerable confusion at the end of lines, where one line rises into another (see Exx. 17, 20).

(15) On the other hand, the need to fill space is satisfied by the *extension* or stretching of letters and ligatures (see Exx. 1 and 2).

(16) Most shekasta deformations have to do more with the need to modify letters that in nasta‘liq curve against the flow of the pen, and so frustrate or check the writer's speed. Examples include final forms that curve up, as in the *bowl* (*da'era*) of *sin*, *shin*, *sad*, *zad*, *ya*, and even *lam* and *nun*, which are therefore commonly extended. This type of extension is an especially common characteristic of shekasta-amiz writing. Two of

these same final forms (*nun* and *ya*) may also be *recurved*. Final *ya* in particular is commonly either uncurved to extend under the following penstroke, or recurved to extend back underneath itself and the penstroke it concluded. Assimilation of the final forms of a number of letters to identical models of extension and recurving may be seen in Example 5 (viz. all the instances here of *sin*, *shin*, *sad*, *zad*, *lam*, and *nun*). Several of these modifications had already been launched in nasta'liq.

(17) Other common features of nasta'liq that are further developed in shekasta include *displacement* and *clustering* of dots: the two dots of a *te* and the single dot of an adjacent *nun* may be written as a three-dot group similar to the dots of a *shin*; or they may appear closer to another letter.

(18) Dots and other diacritics may simply not appear. The dots that conventionally distinguish *shin* from *sin*, *zal* from *dal*, *ze* and *zhe* from *re*, and *te*, *se*, *pe*, and *ya* from *be* are commonly omitted. *Nun* may also lose its dot, as may *jim*, *khe*, *gheyn* and *fe*. *Qaf* also appears without dots. Even the form of *he* that requires a supporting or hanging *hook* (*aviza*) may lose it, and *kaf* may lose its *diagonal* cap (*sarkesh*). (The same is true for *che* and *gaf*, but for much of the period represented in this selection these letters were not normally distinguished from *jim* and *kaf*). The omission of *uprights* (*alef*, *dasta*) in *ta* and *za* is less common, but also occurs.

This wholesale omission of dots and other diacritical points may at first present a difficulty. Although it certainly complicates the decipherment of ambiguous areas of text, a little practice and reflection can overcome most problems. Consider for example that final *qaf* and *fe* are distinguished not only by the number of their dots, but by *qaf*'s deeper bowl; and although the shekasta form of *ast* without dots could also be read as *asp*, the context almost always precludes such ambiguity. Omission of dots and other diacritics may therefore in practice not be a significantly greater challenge than undotted i's and uncrossed t's in English.

(19) The diagnostic shapes of letters are often lost. The *teeth* (*dandana*, *shusha*) of letters such as *sin* or medial *be*, *te*, etc. are smoothed out or simply neglected, with the result that, for example, a *sin* may be distinguished from a *be* only by its length, and sometimes even that is reduced. The *eyelet* (*kala* or *sar*) of *vav*, *mim*, *fe* and *qaf* may also be reduced beyond recognition.

(20) In the case of diacritics, it is worth noting that in some cases there is uncertainty about the precise nature of the standard form. The manuals do not always agree. Dots are of course in origin dots, inherited from pre-nasta'liq styles. Other marks are not, however, always what they now appear to be. The evolution of print fonts has led to rationalization and standardization of some traditional graphs. For example, *hamza*, which resembles a diacritic more than an independent letter in both Persian and Urdu, is in origin the head (*sar*) of an initial *'eyn*. It sometimes appears relaxed and elongated, suggesting a *ya*. However, the optional sign that may be used over final *silent he* (*ha-ye mokhtafi*) to indicate a following *ezafa* is in origin not a hamza but a miniature

representation of the top of an independent *ya* (called *sar-e ya*), showing the pronunciation of ezafa (sc. *-ye*) in that environment. In most fonts, it is represented by hamza, and is perhaps for that reason so called in standard works such as Lambton and Lazard. Similarly, the squiggle that nestles in the dish of a final *kaf* is in origin probably a miniature *kaf*, and was used in place of the diagonal in Persian *kaf* to distinguish it from other letters. Later, when *gaf* was not distinguished by a second diagonal (*sar-kesh*) it was used to distinguish *kaf* from *gaf*. Like *sar-e ya*, it may resemble hamza and in some print fonts it appears to have been assimilated to that character, as in the font used in this volume. In writing it too tends to assume the more relaxed curves of the *sar-e ya*.

(21) A final feature that deserves mention in the category of the modification of nasta‘liq conventions is the tendency for the relative size of individual letters, and consequently their legibility, to be subordinated to the flow of the pen. Some letters are *exaggerated* at the expense of others. Some are *minimized* to the point of being almost invisible, though perhaps suggested by the ligature environment on either side. Good examples of this may be seen in Exx. 1-3, and passim.

II. Specific Penstrokes

(22) Obviously, the routine modifications of letters in shekasta writing go far beyond these simple points that were already conventional, or at least apparent, in calligraphic nasta‘liq. Personal styles involve further idiosyncratic deformations of particular letters, and we have pointed these out in the annotations to the Examples as they occur. But the reader needs to be able to anticipate these forms. Consideration of the most significant differences between handwriting in the Perso-Arabic and Latin scripts may make them easier to anticipate. Consider these three factors:

(a) Most Arabic letters are simpler in form than most Latin letters.

(b) While all Latin letters can be joined fore and aft, seven (over twenty percent of the total of thirty-two) Perso-Arabic letters do not normally connect to a following letter.

(c) While only two Latin letters require diacritics (in English), twenty-one (66%) Perso-Arabic letters require them, seventeen in the form of dots and five in the form of uprights or diagonal strokes; while a twenty-second, *he*, requires one in certain situations.

(d) There are also free-floating diacritics: (i) *fatha, kasra,* and *zamma*, which are used to denote short vowels in cases of possible ambiguity, and (ii) those distinguishing marks discussed above that have largely been assimilated to hamza and appear in certain situations only.

(23) The first of these three factors facilitates streamlining and encourages shortcuts. The second and third are crucial to the relationship between word and penstroke.

Whereas in Latin writing the penstroke is typically coterminous with the word, in correct Perso-Arabic writing (other than shekasta) a non-connecting letter forces the end of a penstroke before the end of the word, with the result that some words need two or more penstrokes, apart from completion with diacritics. The distinguishing feature of shekasta is that it runs non-connecting letters (*alef, dal, zal, re, ze, zhe, vav*) on into the next letter, especially, but not only, within the word.

(24) It should also be noted here that one penstroke may in some cases be run through two or more words. This occurs most commonly with clitics, such as the preposition *ba* and the enclitic pronouns. But extended penstrokes may also flow on further, producing examples where one penstroke comprises two or even more independent words. This phenomenon is especially common in bureaucratic copperplate.

The remainder of this section has to do with common treatments of non-connecting classes of letters in shekasta, with their variation in different environments and with their effects on those environments. The classes of letters are introduced in alphabetical order.

Alef:

(25) Initial *alef* is commonly run on into the following letter, as in *esfahan*. For other instances see *inchonin* (Ex 7:4), *so'al* (11:7) and *az* (32:1). It is often begun with a serif, as in *ast* or *in*.

(26) In the Arabic definite article initial *alef* often appears to begin from the bottom and lead into the *lam* at the top, as in *al-masarrat* (Ex. 8:3), *al-hal* (16:2), *al-kheyr* (17:4), *al-khezr* (30:6), *al-din* (31:3) and *al-'amal* (31:6). This can also occur in the demonstratives *in* and *an* attached to nouns, as in *an-mehraban* (8:7 and 8:15), *inja* (13:13 and 19:9) and *an-janab* (17:4), as though on the model of *be-anjanab*, etc.

(27) In some combinations *alef* assimilates to a pattern that is particularly productive, as in *aban*. See also *asar* (Ex. 22:7), *ro'aya* (32:4), *eqdamat* (35:4), *ayyam* (50:7) and *molaqat* (51:5). This pattern is discussed at length below in no. 43 under *re*-forms. See also *angrezi* (9:1 and elsewhere).

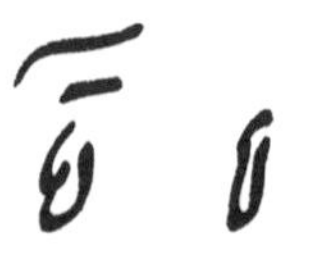

(28) In the case of *aqa* the same pattern has been further simplified to become a logograph.

(29) When initial *alef* follows a non-connecting letter in the middle of a word it is not joined at the bottom like a final *alef* following, say, *be*. Instead, the preceding letter (such as *re*)

runs into a ligature that circles round to connect to the top of *alef* from the left). Cf. *javad, iran* and *qarar.*

(30) A connected *alef* may lead directly into the next letter at the top where it finishes, without regard to the initial alignment of the word, as in *hasel.*

Be-forms:
(31) being connectors, *be*-forms are unremarkable except for their tendency to be minimized to the point of becoming invisible, or to become indistinguishable (especially medially) from *fe, qaf, mim, nun* and even *he.*

Jim-forms:
(32) The *beak* of *jim*-forms appears as a simple loop when a non-connecting letter is led into it, such as *alef* in *ahmad*, or *vav* in *borujerd* (cf. no. 49, below).

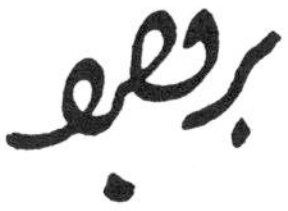

(33) In the initial position *jim*-forms sometimes appear as a more complex figure of eight.

(34) Somewhat more remarkable is the appearance of final *jim*-forms in medial or even sometimes in initial positions, as in these examples. Final *jim* sometimes resembles final *'eyn* (see the remarks on *sad* in no. 52 below).

Dal-forms:
(35) In the initial position *dal* may be started with an exaggerated movement to the right. This distinguishes it from *re*-forms, as in *del*, *dey.*

(36) When followed by *vav* this exaggeration has developed into a standard logograph, which is common in *do, dowlat* and *dust.*

(37) *Dal* may also assimilate to the pattern discussed below in no. 43, as in *mardoman* (Ex. 9:3), *shadmani* (8:24) and *shad-kami* (8:15) and *khodatan* (45:6). See also no. 27 above.

(38) In the medial and final positions *dal* is commonly connected by a loop from the left, as in *shavad* and *barmigardad.* See also *emtedad* (Ex. 8:6) and *dada* (11:3).

(39) *Dal* may simply be connected from above, especially after

alef, as in *bad*.

(40) After *sin*-forms, *dal* may be reduced to a simple recurved hook, as in *shod, bashad* (cf. no. 48, below).

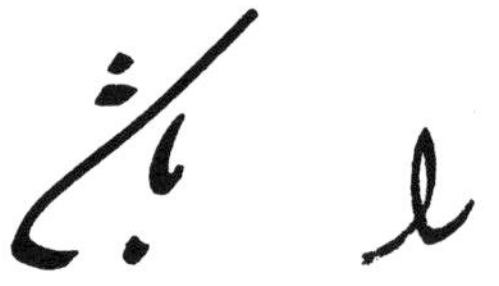

Re-forms:
(41) In the initial position *re* is typically run straight on into the next letter, as in the characteristic shekasta form of the clitic *ra*. See also the *za* of *mirza*.

(42) *re* may also run into a more pronounced ligature before beginning the next letter, as in *ersal*.

(43) *Re*-forms also produce a distinctive tri-literal graph when followed by a *mim*, a letter of the single-tooth medial form (such as *be, te, nun,* or *ye*), followed by an *alef*. For example, the *re-be-alef* of *mehrban* (Ex. 6:6,8) and *darbar* (Ex. 19:1) as a single shekasta penstroke appears identical to the *ze-ye-alef* of *ziyada* and the *re-mim-alef* of *farmayand*. Other sequences that assimilate to the same form include *re-ye-alef* (*esdar yafte*, Ex. 7:3), *dal-ye-alef* (*diyar*, 18:2), *ze-mim-alef* in *molazeman* (18:4), *ze-nun-alef* in *ruznamcha* (38:1), *vav-mim-alef* in *toman* (41:7, 50:2,5, and 54:10), *ze-he-alef* in *ruz-ha* (42:6), *vav-ye-alef* in *va-ya* (46:5) *alef-mim-alef* (*emam*, 19:12). Initial *alef* and *dal* may also assimilate to this pattern (see the combinations *alef-be-alef, alef-mim-alef, alef-qaf-alef, alef-ye-alef, dal-te-alef, dal-kaf-alef* and *dal-mim-alef* above, nos. 27 and 37).

(44) In the medial position the beginning of *re* in some words is exaggerated by a turn that may even move slightly to the right, rather than moving straight on as would be normal in nasta'liq. Examples include *mardom, baraye* and *izadi*.

(45) *Re* may appear as a simple upright stroke, similar to a *lam* without the bowl, as in Ex. 47:2. See also *zabardasti* (Ex. 9:4), *midarad* (11:4), *pardazad* (11:7), *davazdah* (13:12), *madarej* (22:11), *vared* (32:10, 47:2), *nadarad* (34:19) and *darad* (47:6).

(46) Medial *re* may sometimes seem to be lost between two other letters, as in *gardad* (Ex. 8:15) and *'arz* (17:8).

Sin/shin:
(47) Apart from loss of teeth, which is common in nasta'liq

generally, in the initial position these forms sometimes appear almost vertical, as in *shavam*, and may be reduced to become indistinguishable from *be*-forms.

(48) The combination *sin* or *shin* with *dal* may be written as a logograph (cf. above no. 40). See also *bashad* in Ex. 13:15. *Sana* may also be written the same way (cf. 6:1).

Sad/zad:
(49) When entered from a non-connector, the loop of *sad* may be indistinguishable from the *jim*-form in no. 32, above (cf. *vosul*), except for the following diagnostic tooth.

(50) The diagnostic tooth is often streamlined, as in *razi*.

Ta/za:
(51) The loop of a *ta*, whether or not it retains its diacritic upright, may engulf the following letter if it is a medial form, as in *tehran*. See also *ezhar* in Ex. 37:2, 7.

'Eyn/gheyn:
(52) The open jaw that distinguishes the initial form of these letters makes them relatively less susceptible to deformation, but the lower curve of the final form is sometimes written in initial positions, as in *'Ali*. Cf. the similiar usage for *jim*-forms in no. 34, above.

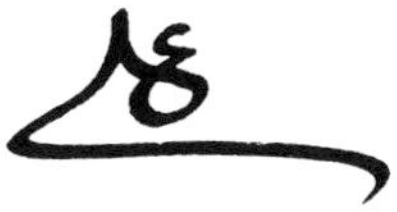

Fe/qaf:
(53) Although distinguished in the final position by the fact that *fe* has a *be*-form bowl, while the bowl of *qaf* approximates that of *lam*, in initial and medial positions these forms are indistinguishable except by the number of diacritic dots. However the dots may be omitted and the letters minimized to the point of being indistinguishable from *be*-forms.

(54) They may be reduced to the intermediate point of the graph described in no. 43, above.

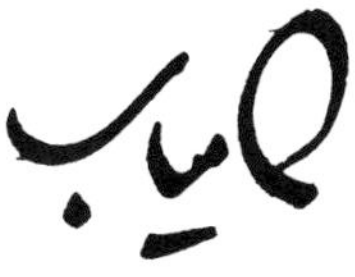

Kaf/gaf:
(55) The diagonal of initial *kaf* may be written as an extension of a following *alef* in a manner that suggests a figure-of-eight, or even a circle, as in *kava* and *kamyab*.

(56) The conjunction *ke* is further deformed into a standard

logograph which simply curves back on itself.

(57) Medially, the bearer of the diacritic diagonal(s) may be minimized to the point of not being distinguishable.

(58) The diagonal is occasionally omitted.

Lam:
(59) The upright stroke of *lam* may barely rise above the level of a *be*-form hook.

(60) The bowl of a final *lam* may be extended, as in *ehtemal* where the *lam* is entered from the top of the *alef.*

Mim:
(61) Between *dal*- or *re*-forms and a following *alef, mim* is commonly reduced to a notch on an upward stroke. See above, no. 43.

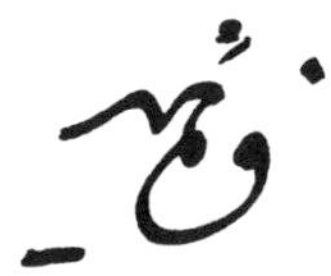

(62) The notch of medial *mim* is sometimes exaggerated downwards, as in *Mohammad* (Ex. 9:1).

(63) In the final position the eyelet may be minimized, leaving only the vertical downward stroke or tail.

Nun:
(64) *Nun* is treated identically to *be*-forms in initial and medial positions. Like other members of this form it may disappear entirely or be represented only by its diacritic dot, especially in the third-person verbal inflection, as in *beravand* (Ex. 32:4).

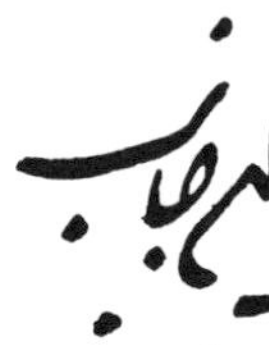

(65) In the final position it may be extended, recurved, or normal (with the top sometimes almost closed) whether or not is it entered from the preceding letter.

Vav:
(66) When *vav* is run into the following letter there is a tendency to exaggerate its head, as in *avval, beravad, qabul* and *vosul*, which has the effect of distinguishing it from *re*-forms but making it difficult to distinguish from *dal*-forms.

(67) It is also worth noting that when *vav* is run into a final *ya*, rather than run directly into it, the pen rises to begin the *ya*, as in *akhavi*.

He:

(68) In all positions *he* tends to be simplified to the point where it is difficult to distinguish. Whether or not this produces ambiguity, the diacritic supporting hook is often added even in positions where in nasta'liq it would not be expected. It is worth noting that the hook that supports *he* is in origin an integral part of the letter: one of the two loops of the original figure of eight disappeared in the process of streamlining, and was added underneath as a diacritic.

(69) Initial *he* is usually written as in nasta'liq (see *hadi*). When it occurs medially or is entered directly from the preceding letter the following *alef* is usually curled round to the right. See *dehat* and *cahar*, and cf. no. 43, above.

(70) In other combinations *he* usually appears as an inverse, or downward, tooth, as in *cahar*.

(71) In final positions it may take the form of a circle at the end of a *dal*- or *re*-form, as in *banda*. See also *namuda* in Ex. 10:5; the same example contains further instances.

(72) In the same position, instead of closing the circle the pen may curve upwards, as in *ba-'alava*. For other instances see *payanda* (Ex. 7:5), *bahra-var* (7:6), *dar-manda* (7:9), *mastura* (8:9), *erada* (8:13), *chehra* (8:15), *faqara* (35:3) and *rah* (47:4).

(73) Even in this final position *he* often takes the diacritic hook, as in *deh*.

(74) As the pen moves back to place the diacritic hook it often makes the *he* appear to recurve back under the preceding letter and the hook therefore appears to relate to the preceding letter, as in *karda, aluda* and *farmuda*.

(75) Final *he* also appears as a simple recurved hook without the supporting diacritic, as in *zello-ho* (Ex. 24:1) and *shoda* (24:4).

Ya:
(76) Initial and medial *ya* are treated similarly to *be*-forms.

(77) Apart from extension and recurving, final *ya* receives one other treatment worthy of mention: it is sometimes written inside the previous letter: see examples *chubi* (Ex. 9:5), *chavoni* (10:3).

(78) In all these Examples the flow of the pen appears always to take precedence over other considerations, except that where legibility is judged to be at risk the flow may be interrupted in order to restore it by means of a diacritic. In some cases the deformations became standardized to the point where they in turn generated new types of distinguishing feature to help the reader. Additional diacritics, such as three dots under a *sin*, a small numeral 3 above a toothless *sin*, and a hook under a form of *he* that does not require it, began to appear. It is important to remember, however, that such diacritics are designed for the benefit of the colleague who is professionally familiar with related contexts, and are not necessarily helpful for the inexperienced modern reader. Since the 1960s when public education was extended throughout Iran (and to a lesser extent in Afghanistan and in South Asia), writing habits, including the variety of deformations, have diversified.

III. Numerical Notation

The Examples in this book illustrate four features of numerical notation that may be unfamiliar:

(79) The Arabic numeral for seven, which is generally known in its upright V-form, is in South Asia commonly written pointing to the left, rotated to the right through ninety degrees.

(80) Typically numbers are written out, and the numerals are added above. Dates are discussed in no. 12 above.

(81) The numerical values of the Semitic letters, known generally in languages using the Arabic script as the *abjad* (from the first four letters of the old Semitic alphabet from which it derives) appear not infrequently, but mostly in standard formulas (see illustrations on the next three pages). The most conspicuous instance is in Ex. 4, from a manuscript of the *Akhlaq-e Jalali* written in 1870, in which the number twelve occurs eight times to signify the sum of the letters *he* (value = 8) and *dal* (value = 4) of *hadd*, meaning limit or end (sc. of a discussion), to mark the end of marginal notes.

(82) Finally, some discussion is needed here of the system of numerical notation known variously as *siyaq* (most commonly in Persian), *siyaqat* (generally in Ottoman Turkish) or *raqam* (in South Asia). This notation is derived from the Arabic names of the numerals. The graphs themselves are stylized versions of the initial penstrokes of the

Arabic words for one, two, three, etc. Once the basic principle is understood, the graphs are relatively simple to read so long as they are clearly written. However, as with shekasta the forms tend to suffer deformation at the hands of professional writers and accountants. Furthermore, there is some regional variation in usage between South Asia, Iran, Istanbul, and Cairo. This is illustrated below where a South Asian and an Iranian version are reproduced for comparison. Differences in style are further complicated by the South Asian preference for *‘adad* and *‘adadan* over *wahed* and *ithnayn* (which are normal in Iran and further west) as the basis for 1 and 2. For the numbers 11-19 the symbol for 10 is written with the characteristic feature of each unit extended underneath, and so on up to 100, which is recognisable as the first penstroke of the Arabic word for a hundred, and so on into the thousands and beyond. The hundreds are written to the right of the tens which are written over the units. Siyaq belongs to the realms of both commerce and administration, especially accounting and tax and land records. It was taught in schools in Iran until the early 1930s and is still in use in commerce and agricultural administration. Siyaq notations appear in Exx. 50 and 72.

ابجد هوز حطی کلمن

۱ ۲ ۳ ۴ ۵ ۶ ۷ ۸ ۹ ۱۰ ۲۰ ۳۰ ۴۰ ۵

سعفص قرشت ثخذ ضظغ

۶۰ ۷۰ ۸۰ ۹۰ ۱۰۰ ۲۰۰ ۳۰۰ ۴۰۰ ۵۰۰ ۶۰۰ ۷۰۰ ۸۰۰ ۹۰۰ ۱۰۰۰

Abjad Table with the Numerical Values of the Letters
Majidi, Mohammad-Reza, *Das arabisch-persische Alphabet in den Sprachen der Welt.* Hamburg, 1984, p. 139.

الف	١	ز	٧	ق	١٠٠
ب	٢	س	٦٠	ک	٢٠
ت	٤٠٠	ش	٣٠٠	ل	٣٠
ث	٥٠٠	ص	٩٠	م	٤٠
ج	٣	ض	٨٠٠	ن	٥٠
ح	٨	ط	٩	و	٦
خ	٦٠٠	ظ	٩٠٠	ه ـ ه	٥
د	٤	ع	٧٠	ی	١٠
ذ	٧٠٠	غ	١٠٠٠		
ر	٢٠٠	ف	٨٠		

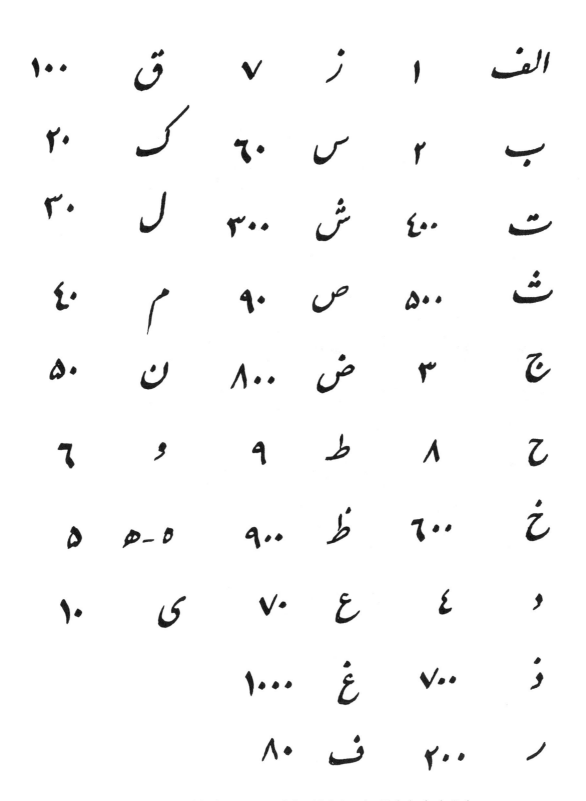

Abjad Table with the Letters of the Alphabet in Alphabetical Order
with their Abjad Numerical Equivalents

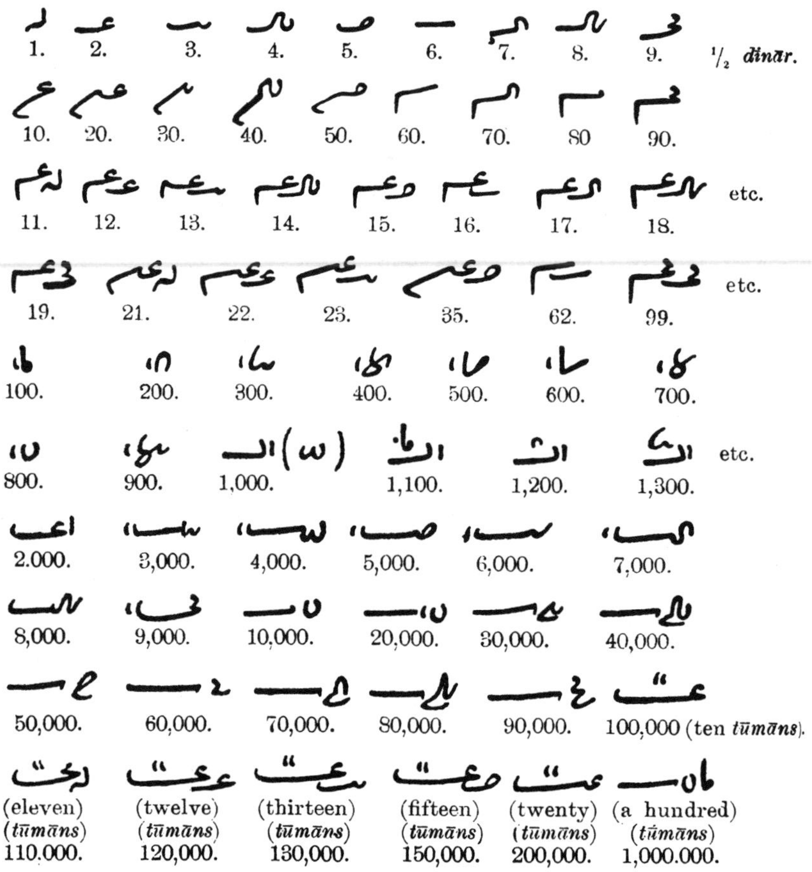

Representative Paradigm of Siyaq Forms Used in Iran
St. Clair-Tisdall, 1923, p. 220.

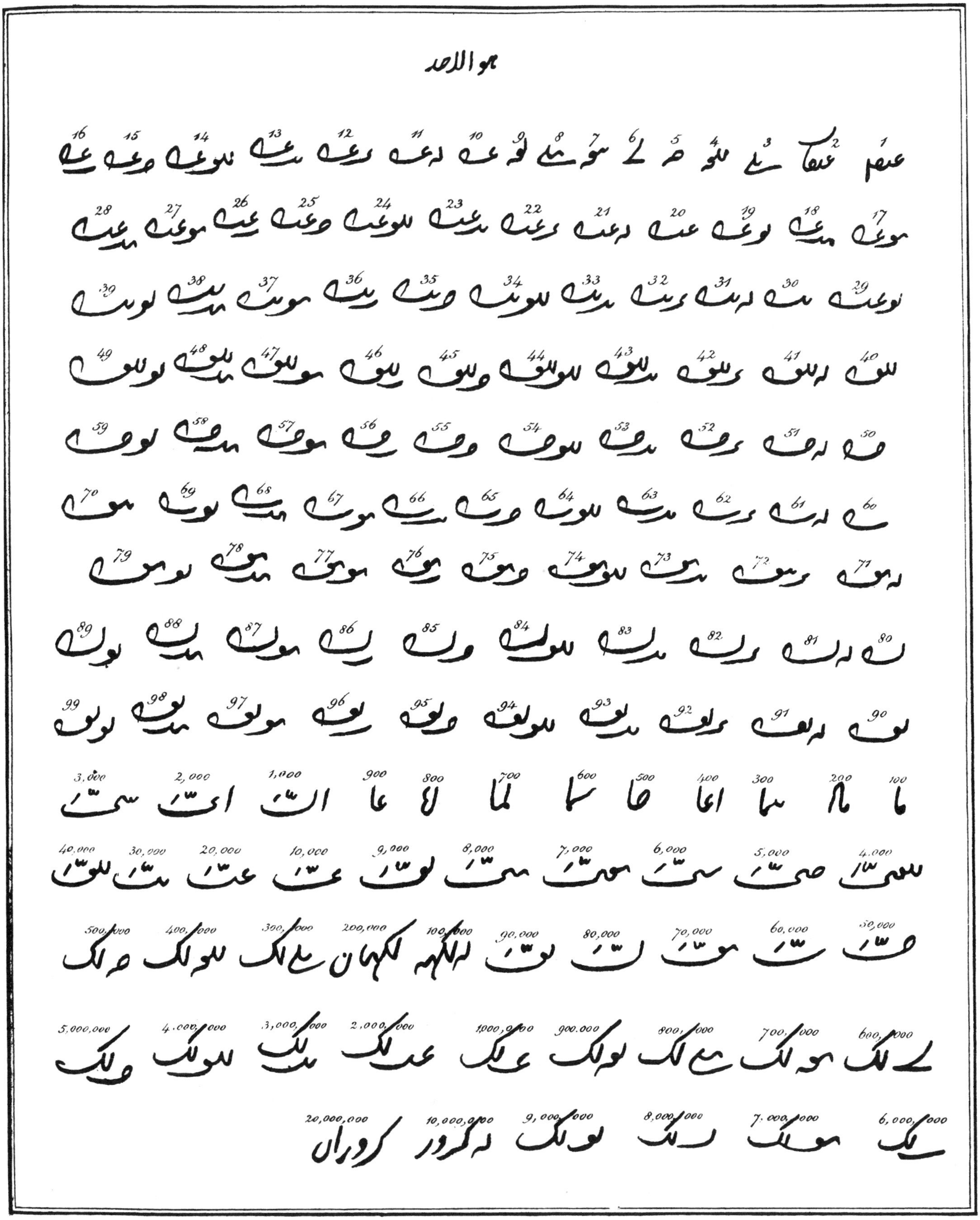

Representative Paradigm of Siyaq Forms Used in India
Stewart 1825, pl. 7

IV. Abbreviations

Epithets

صلعم	صلی الله علیه و سلم
ص	صلی الله علیه و سلم
صم	The shekasta form of the above signs
عم	علیه السلام یا علیهم السلام
ع	Shortened form of the above
رض	رضی الله عنه یا عنهم
	رضوان الله علیه
ره	رحمة الله علیه
قده	قدس سره
انشا	ان شاءالله
عج	عجل الله فرجه
لعم	لعنت الله علیه

Titles of Some Important Books of *feqh*

کا یا فی	کافی ثقة الاسلام کلینی
یب	تهذیب الاحکام شیخ طوسی
ط	المبسوط شیخ طوسی
یه	النهایة شیخ طوسی
ف	کتاب الخلاف شیخ طوسی
من	من لایحضره الفقیه صدوق ابن بابویه
الفقیه	the same
سر	السرائر ابن ادریس
یع	شرایع الاسلام محقق حلی
یر	تحریر الاحکام علامه ابن مطهر حلی
ة	تنصرة و تذکرة علامه ابن مطهر حلی
لف	المختلف علامه ابن مطهر حلی

س	الدروس شهيد اول
ضه	روضة البهيّه (معروف به شرح لمعه) شهيد ثانى
ئق	الحدائق الناضرة بحرانى

Abbreviations Commonly Used in Books of *feqh*

المطـ	المطلق	مطـ	مطلقا
الظ یا الظم	فى الظاهر يا الظاهر	ظ	ظاهراً يا ظاهر
ایضـ	ايضا	المصـ	المصنف
المحـ	المحال	محـ	محال
المشـ	المشهور	الخ	الى آخر
تمـ	تمت	کک یا کک	كذالك

Numerical Representations According to Abjad Values.

١١٠ : على	٩٢ : محمد
١١٨ : حسن	١٢١ : يا على
٧٨٦ : بسم الله الرحمن الرحيم	١٢٨ : حسين
٢٤٦٨ يا ٨٦٤٢ : بدوح	١٢ : حدّ

For a discussion of بدوح see Henri Cotelle, "Explication du mot بدوح." *Journal Asiatique* 4e série, 12 (1848):521–25, and Dozy, R., *Supplement*, s.v. بدوح.

Lunar Months

ع ۱	ربيع الاول	ع ۲	ربيع الثانى
ج ۱	جمادى الاولىٰ	ج ۲	جمادى الثانى
ذق	ذى قعدة الحرام	ذج	ذى حجّه الحرام

Other Indications of Time

ش	سال شمسی	ق	سال قمری
م یا ب.م	بعد از میلاد مسیح	ق.م	قبل از میلاد مسیح

Parts of Books

ص	صفحه	صص	صفحات
ح	حاشیه	ع	مصرع

I

The five calligraphic examples that follow represent basic forms of nasta'liq and shekasta from which all the rest of our examples derive. These are, in a sense, timeless, since they are written in a consciously disciplined manner according to precepts based on aesthetic standards, and can be reproduced at any time by a trained calligrapher.

Examples in this group are taken from Welch 1979, Meredith-Owens 1973, Safadi 1979, Davani 1307, and a *nowruz* card written in the 1980s.

سیامک خجسته یکی پور داشت | که نزد نیا جای دستور داشت

نیا پروریده مر او را ببر | بنزد نیا یادکار پدر

چو بنهاد دل کینه و جنک را | بخواند آن کرانمایه هوشنک را

که من لشکری کرد خواهم همی | خروشی برآورد خواهم همی

١ سیامك خجسته یکی پور داشت که نزد نیا جای دستور داشت
٢ نیا پروریده مر اورا ببر بنزد نیا یادکار پدر
٣ چو بنهاد دل کینه و جنك را بخواند آن کرانمایه هوشنك را
٤ که من لشکری کرد خواهم همی خروشے بآورد خواهم همی

Welch 1979, pl. 1. From a manuscript of Ferdowsi's *Shahnama* written in Isfahan, ca. 1522.

Notes

This first example is from an early Safavid manuscript and its script can be taken as typical of calligraphic practice of the time in nasta'liq. Since it is poetry, the half-lines are spatially organized to match each other, which occasions some examples of cramming, stacking, and especially extension. The following points should be noted:

(a) Certain letters are exaggerated beyond their normal proportions, such as the س of دستور in line 1, or the ش of لشکری in line 4.

(b) Other letters are minimized, such as the ز of بنزد in line 2, or the final ه of کینه in line 3.

(c) Diacritics are employed, such as a small ک in the dish of the کاف of سیامك in line 1, or the three dots under the س of دستور to improve legibility where it may be compromised by exaggeration or by variation of form (in this case the writing of س without teeth).

(d) Some parts of letters are lost, such as the hook of initial ه in خواهم and همی in line 4.

(e) Variations on basic letter-forms appear, such as the س that lacks teeth, the recurved final ی in line 4, and the lengthening of letters such as ی in نیا and ب in ببر in line 2.

(f) ک and گ, ج and چ, ز and ژ, and ب and پ are not always distinguished.

(g) Some forms are assimilated to a pattern and stand out on the page looking very similar, such as the bowl of س and the dish of ت and ک in line 1, and similarly for ن, ب, and ی in line 2.

(h) To save space or create a straight left margin, parts of words or whole words may be stacked at the end of lines, such as داشت in line 1, را in line 3, and همی in line 4.

(i) Finally, dots can be displaced, generally to the left, as in ببر in line 2 or کینه in line 3. These points are discussed above in the Guide.

Line by line:

2: as noted, the ی of نیا is lengthened (as نیـــا): compare the closely-written version of the same word in 2. The ر of ببر is minimized when compared with the ر of را just below in line 3. The ن of بنزد is lengthened (as بنـــزد) and the ز is proportionally the same size as the final ر of line 2. The گ of یادگار is written without a second diagonal stroke; see also گرانمایه and هوشنگ in line 3.

3: the ه of هوشنگ lacks a lower hook.

4: the recurved ی of خروشی has two dots under it. The ا of باآورد has an optional madda.

یار شد با من بیکجا مار زشت
تا بیفتادم بخواری از بهشت

چون بدل کردند خلوت جای من
تخته بند پای من شد پاچی من

عزم آن دارم کزین تاریک جای
رهبری باشد بخلدم رهنمای

من نه آن مرغم که در پسلطان رسم
بس بود انیم که در دربان رسم

کی بود سیمرغ را پروای من
بس بود فردوس اعلی جای من

من ندارم در جهان کار دگر
تا بهشتم ره دهد بار دگر

١	یار شد با من بیکجا مار زشت	تا بیفتادم بخواری از بهشت
٢	جون بدل کردند خلوت جای من	تخته بند پای من شد پای من
٣	عزم آن دارم کزین تاریك جای	رهبری باشد بخلدم رهنمای
٤	من نه آن مرغم که در سلطان رسم	بس بود اینم که در دربان رسم
٥	کی بود سیمرغ را پروای من	بس بود فردوس اعلی جای من
٦	من ندارم در جهان کار دکر	تا بهشتم ره دهد بار دکر

Meredith–Owens 1973, pl. 12. From a manuscript of 'Attar's *Manteq al-Teyr*, written in Herat, 1490–1500.

Notes

This passage shows further examples of the features illustrated in the previous example, in particular displacement and omission of dots and other diacritics.

Line by line:

1: the dots of the ش of شد are displaced to the right. The dot of the ب of بیکجا is lacking. The dot of the ز of زشت is displaced to the right.

2: چون is written as جون. In تخته the dots of خ and ت are clustered in a triangle.

3: the ی of کزین lacks dots. The تا of تاریك is stacked above the ن of کزین. The ه of رهبری and of رهنمای lacks the hook. The با of باشد is stacked above the ی of رهبری, and its dot is displaced to the left.

4: the س of سلطان and of بس lack teeth and have three dots underneath. بود is stacked over the س of بس, but its dot is below.

5: the ی of کی meets the following ب of بود. The س of سیمرغ and of فردوس lack teeth and have three dots underneath. The ی of سیمرغ lacks dots.

6: the ند of ندارم is stacked over the ن of من. دگر is written as دکر.

فراغت دارد از تلخی لبانش
که از شکر تنک آمد دهانش

١ سکر با کلشکر آمیز کرده ز تلخیہا لبش پرہیز کرده
٢ فی شہور سنه ١٠٣٤

٣ فراغت دارد از تلخی لبانش که از شکر بتنك آمد دہانش

٤ تحریرا فی بلده الکشمیر
٥ بہر ہنکامه کو رخسار بنمود ز خوبان ہیچکس دیدار ننمود
٦ فقیر محمّد درویش السمرقندے غفر له

Safadi 1979, pl. 113.

Notes

This example further illustrates a number of variations on omission and displacement of dots, omission of the hook of initial ه, extension of ligatures, and the addition of diacritics. Each panel contains a single line of poetry, and there are notes in panels 1 and 3.

Line by line:

1: the dots of the ش of شکر are lacking. The گ of گلشکر is written as ک. The ی of تلخیها and the پ of پرهیز lack dots. The ه of پرهیز lacks its hook.

2: the س of سنه has three dots under it.

3: the خ of تلخی lacks its dot. The ن of لبانش has no distinguishing tooth before the ش: see also دهانش in line 3 and بس in Ex. 2:4. The dots of ب and ن in بتنگ are displaced to the left, and the dot of the ن is over the گ. The ها of دهانش is written as two hooks stacked vertically. There appears to be a hamza under the final ش of دہانش.

4: there appears to be an unexplained hamza below the first ر of تحریراً. The ا lacks the tanvin.

5: the initial ه of هنگامه lacks the hook. The tooth of the ن is nearer to the

گ than to the ه. The م is reduced to a tooth. گ is written as ک. The س of رخسار has three dots under it. The ه of هیچکس lacks its hook. The ی lacks dots. The س has three dots under it.

6: in فقیر, the dots of the ف and ق are clustered in a triangle and the ی lacks dots. The س of السمرقندی has three dots under it and the final ی is recurved and has two dots underneath. The mark over the غ of غفر, where a zamma might be expected, resembles a hamza.

بعد ازانکه دیگران دست باز کشیده باشند تعلّل نماید تا اگر کسی را بقیت علتی
باشد حجاب نکند و اگر در میان طعام بآب احتیاج افتد بآهستگی بیاشامد چنانکه
آواز دهن و حلق باو نشنوند و در نظر جماعت خلال نکند و آنچه بزبان از دندان
بیرون آرد بخورد واما آنچه بخلال برآید بجائی اندازد که مردم را نفرت نشود و بوقت
دست شستن در پاک کردن انگشتان و بیخ ناخن جهد بلیغ نماید و همچنین در لب و دهن
و دندان و آب دهن در طشت نیندازد و چون آب که دهن بآن شسته باشد
ریزد دست بپوشد و در دست شستن پیش از طعام بر دیگران سبقت نجوید اما
باید که مهماندار در دست شستن پیش از طعام بر دیگران سابق شود لمعه پنجم
در رعایت حقوق پدران و مادران چون بمقتضای عقل و نقل شکر منعم واجبست
و بعد از نعم الهی هیچ نعمت در حق فرزندان چون نعمت پدر و مادر نیست چه پدر
سبب صوری وجود اوست و بعد از ان وسیله تربیت او بتهیه اغذیه والبسه وضروریات
که سبب بقای او و بلوغ بکمال نشو و نماست و باز واسطه حصول کمالات نفسانی ازو

۵۷ و این معنی بر طهارت ذات و لطافت صفات و علو نسب دلیلی ظاهر و حجتی باهر است ۱۲ ۵۸ که اول آن ۳

۱ بعد از انکه دیگران دست باز کشیده باشند تعلل (۱) نماید تا اگر کسے را بقیت رغبتے

۲ باشد حجاب نکند و اگر در میان طعام بآب احتیاج افتد بآہستگی بیاشامد چنانکه

۳ آواز دہن و حلق او نشنوند (۲) و در نظر جماعت خلال (۳) نکند و انچه بزبان از دندان

٤ بیرون آرد بخورد اما انچه بخلال براید بجائی اندازد که مردم را نفرت (٤) نشود و بوقت

۵ دست شستن در پاک کردن انگشتان و بیخ ناخن جهد بلیغ نماید و ہمچنین در لب و دہن

٦ و دندان و آب دہن در طشت (۵) نیندازد و چون آب که دہن بآن شسته باشد

۷ ریزد به دست (٦) بپوشد و در دست شستن پیش از طعام بر دیگران سبقت نجوید اما

۸ باید که مہماندار در دست شستن پیش از طعام بر دیگران سابق شود لمعۂ پنجم

۹ در رعایت حقوق (۷) پدران و مادران چون بمقتضای عقل و نقل شکر منعم واجبست

۱۰ و بعد از نعم (۸) الہی ہیچ نعمت در حق فرزندان چون نعمت پدر و مادر نیست چه پدر

۱۱ سبب صوری وجود اوست و بعد از ان وسیلۂ تربیت او به تہیۂ (۹) اغذیه و البسه و ضروریات

۱۲ که سبب بقای او و بلوغ بکمال نشو و نماست و باز واسطۂ حصول کمالات نفسانے او

Now read in the margins, beginning at the upper left. The line numbers in the following transcription are those of the footnotes, not of the lines as above.

۱ تعلل بر وزن تفعل علت انگیختن و سبب پرسیدن و معنی تاخیر و بہانه جوئے از ان مراد باشد و در کتابی نوشته که حجت انگیختن چون باعث درنگ و تاخیر میشود لہذا مجازا بمعنی درنگ و تاخیر مستعمل میشود و باصطلاح اطبا اندک اندک خوردن چیزی را ۱۲ غیاث

۲ و بسیار ننوشد و کوزه بدست راست گیرد و بسم الله گوید و اولا در کوزه بنگرد تا

حیوانی و خاشاکی نباشد و چنان احتیاط کند که آب از کوزه بر جای نچکد ۱۲

٣ خلال بکسر بمعنی در میان و فاصله و دوستی کردن و دوستان و خصلتها مصدر از باب
مفاعلة و بمعنی چوب دندان و خس و کاه ظاهرا باینمعنی مجازست از غیاث

٤ و کاسه پاک کند بانگشت که در خبرست ہر که کاسه پاک لیسد و پاک خورد آنچنان بود
که بنده آزاد کرده باشد ۱۲

٥ و کلیه در اکثر این ہمه امور آنکه انچه از دیگران نا پسندیده دارد خود ارتکاب آن
نکند ۱۲

٦ و چنان برفق بریزد که بکسی نرسد و در جمله این آداب اخبار و آثار آمده است و
فرق میان آدمی و بہیمه بہمین آداب ست که بہیمه بر مقتضای طبع خورد و نیکو از
زشت نشناسد که اورا این تمیز نداده اند و بکار چون آدمی را این تمیز داده اند و
بکار ندارد حق نعمت عقل و تمیز نگزارده باشد و کفر ان نعمت کرده ۱۲ کذا فے
کیمیاے سعادت

٧ و اینمعنی بر طہارت ذات و لطافت صفات و علو نسب و حسب دلیلی ظاہر و حجتی
باہرست ۱۲

٨ که اول آن (vertically up the side of the page) وجود باشد و بعد لوازم آن که لا
تعد و لا تحصے ست ۱۲

٩ تہیه بفتح اول و کسر ہای ہوز و فتح یای مشدد آمادگی کردن   اغذیه بفتح اول و
کسر ذال معجمه و فتح تحتانی جمع غذا   و البسه بر وزن اغذیه جمع لباس   نشو
و نما ہر دو لفظ بفتح نون ست بمعنی روئیدن و بالیدن ۱۲ غیاث اللغات

Davani 1307, p. 220.

Notes

This hand is typical of lithographed texts of the late 19th century from India. Whereas Exx. 1–3 represent the script as art, this is a pre-typesetting script. It is a clear nasta'liq with no special ligatures or combinations. The footnotes are arranged in the margins around the text. What difficulties there are result from cramming.

Note the distinctions in size of the writing: standard size for the body of the text, larger script for chapter headings or major changes of topic (see line 8, and line 6 of the marginal notes), and smaller writing for the notes and comments written around the text in the margins. It is worth noting that the text in the margin runs in the opposite direction from that of Exx. 31, 32, 34, and 35 which are all personal letters (cf. Ex. 69). The notes continue horizontally across the bottom of the page and then vertically up the right side. The symbol under the superscript numerals in the text and in the notes, a horizontal line with a loop to the left (not represented in the transcription), is a reduced form of نمره. A special symbol in footnote ۸ signals the end of the horizontal line of footnotes and the beginning of the vertical line. In the lower left corner of the page is the catchword چون, indicating the first word of the following page. Catchwords (ترک) were inserted to help binders bind the pages in the correct order: see also Exx. 65:9 and 69:17. The numeral ۱۲, which appears at the end of most marginal notes, is the abjad value of *hadd*, meaning "end"; see also Ex. 70:10 and Guide II.

Changes of topic are indicated by a short overline (e.g., line 2; represented in the transcription by space). It is normal for words to be stacked at the end of a line. Many maddas are missing. Occurrences of final ی in the main text are about evenly divided between normal and recurved, while most are normal in the marginal notes. In Indian usage, the numeral ۷ lies on its side, pointing to the left. There is a superfluous dot at the end of line 1 and over حصول in line 12, and elsewhere scattered throughout the text. غیاث اللغات is an early 19th-century Persian dictionary that was compiled in India.

Line by line:

8: there is a hamza over پنجم where a zamma would be expected (cf. Ex. 3:6).

ز کوی یار می‌آید نسیم باد نوروزی
از این باد ار مدد خواهی چراغ دل برافروزی

چو گل گر خرده‌ای داری خدا را صرف عشرت کن
که قارون را غلط‌ها داد سودای زراندوزی

سخن در پرده می‌گویم چو گل از غنچه بیرون آی
که بیش از پنج روزی نیست حکم میر نوروزی

میی دارم چو جان صافی و صوفی می‌کند عیبش
خدایا هیچ عاقل را مبادا بخت بدروزی

طریق کام بخشی چیست ترک کام خود کردن
کلاه سروری آن است کز این ترک بردوزی

ندانم نوحهٔ قمری به طرف جویبار از چیست
مگر او نیز همچون من غمی دارد شبانروزی

جدا شد یار شیرینت کنون تنها نشین ای شمع
که حکم آسمان این است اگر سازی و گر سوزی

به بستان شو که از بلبل رموز عشق گیری یاد
به مجلس آی کز حافظ غزل گفتن بیاموزی

١ ز کوی یار میآید نسیم باد نوروزی
ازین باد ار مدد خواهی چراغ دل بر افروزی
٢ چو گل گر خرده ای داری خدارا صرف عشرت کن
که قارون را غلط ها داد سودای زر اندوزی
٣ سخن در پرده میگویم چو گل از غنچه بیرون آی
که بیش از پنج روزی نیست حُکم میر نوروزی
٤ میی دارم چو جان صافی و صوفی میکند عیبش
خدایا هیچ عاقل را مبادا بخت بد روزی
٥ طریق کام بخشی چیست ترک کام خود کردن
کلاه سر وری آنست کز این ترک بر دوزی
٦ ندانم نوحهٔ قمری به طرف جویبار از چیست
مگر او نیز همچون من غمی دارد شبانروزی
٧ جدا شد یار شیرینت کنون تنها نشین ای شمع
که حُکم آسمان این است اگر سازی و گر سوزی
٨ به بستان شو که از بلبل رموز عشق گیری یاد
به مجلس آی کز حافظ غزل گفتن بیاموزی

A ghazal of Hafez, from a *nowruz* card written during the 1980s.

Notes

This example displays many of the distinguishing characteristics of shekasta in a clear and consistent calligraphic style. There appear, for example: extension and recurving of final letters, the connecting of letters that by the basic rules of Arabic script should not connect to the left, as in خواهی and چراغ in line 1, را in line 2, and the logograph for که. In addition to these, other features such as exaggeration, minimization, omission of dots and hooks, displacement of dots, and lengthening of letters, also appear. Several letters that appear in their extended form are assimilated to a common pattern; see also Ex. 52. For a discussion of this point, see Guide no. 16 and Faza'eli 1971, p. 640 (see also Ex. 52). The diagonal of ک often misses the upright and extends past it. ک and گ are distinguished, and an effort has been made to include all relevant dots.

Line by line:

1: the و of کوی is connected to the following ی. The dot of the ز of نوروزی is to the left of the final extended ی. The و of خواهی is connected to the following ا, as is the ر of چراغ.

2: the ل of گل is extended and barely rises vertically. The ف of صرف is superposed. که is written as a logograph: this form also appears in lines 3, 7, and 8. The ر of را is connected to the following ا, which is typical in shekasta. The writing of the ها of غلط ها as two hooks stacked vertically is also a convention in this style, but the separation of ها from غلط is unconventional.

3: the last four words are stacked, and in order to achieve a desired spatial arrangement their final letters remain unextended.

5: the diagonal of the ک of ترک runs into the diacritic ک of ترک. The و of خود is connected to the following د. The diagonal of the ک of کز runs into the dot of the ز.

6: the dot of the ز in نیز is missing. The ا in شبانروزی is minimized (also in بستان in line 8) .

8: the ن of بستان is extended and superposed. The final ل of بلبل is extended and barely rises vertically. The د of یاد is superposed.

II

The following twenty examples, from the eighteenth and early nineteenth centuries, were written mostly in India. They are divided into two sub-sections: In the first, a prominent line across the top of the page marks the beginning of the formal part of the text and usually follows a date and a salutation. In the second, this overlining is absent. Although this grouping is based on a formal feature, it also reflects the fact that those examples with a line are official documents and those lacking it are private letters.

Examples in this group are all drawn from Stewart 1825.

۲۲

جواب خط الماس علیخان بهادر مرقومهٔ بیست و دوم ماه دسمبر ۱۸۰۱ع مطابق
یازدهم شهر شعبان ۱۲۱۶ هجری شرح آنکه مکاتبه تودد انتما متضمن خبر ورود
و خورسندی خاطر از دریافت مژده ورود جناب مستطاب معلی القاب
لارد صاحب بهادر دام اقباله و همرکاب بودن مخلص و عدم رسیدن
خود در الهآباد بسبب ضعف و ناتوانی ها و غیره مراتب نگاشته و ارتحال عم معظم
مسمی خلد منزلت راجه صاحب مهربان راجه بهوانی پرشاد و حصول مسرت مشمول
نموده سرور و مندرجه نامه مفاوضات سطوع ساخته در باب ضعف و ناتوانی
آن مهربان که مانع حصول مسرت ملاقات گشته شد موجب حسرت خاطر گردید
انشاءالله تعالی در اثنای راه مقام کانپور بزودی ایام از مواصلت صوری
خورسند بهار حصول خواهد انجامید و از ملاقات راجه صاحب موصوف
مسرور گشت و حسب الارقام آن مهربان راجه موصوف بدولت
ملازمت حضور نواب صاحب ممدوح فایز گردانید و عرض مرسوله نیز
از دست آن بمطالعه گذشته جواب حاصل شده میرود از آن
مراتب تفصیلات اینسرکار واضح خواهد گردید بر صدق مخلص
پیوسته خواهان خیریتها انگاشته یاد دست داد مواصلت صوری
باز نامه مکاتبات بهجت آیات مسرور و مبتهج مینموده باشند زیاده

١ جوابخط الماس عليخان بهادر مرقومه بيست و دوم ٢٢ ماه دسنمبر سنه ١٨٠١
عيسوى مطابق
٢ بانزدہم شهر شعبان سنه ١٢١٦ ہجرى شرح آنكه مكاتبه تودد افزا متضمن بر سرور
٣ و خورسندى خاطر از دريافت مژده ورود جناب مستطاب معلے القاب
٤ لارد صاحب بهادر دام اقباله و ہمركاب بودن مخلص و عدم رسيدن
٥ خود در اله آباد بسبب ضعف و ناتوانے ہا و غيره مراتب يكانكيت و اتحاد معه عرضى
٦ رسمى حضور معرفت راجه صاحب مهربان راجه بهوانے برشاد وصول مسرت شمول
٧ نموده مسرور و بمندرجه ہا مفصل مطلع ساخت دريافت ضعف و ناتوانے
٨ آن مهربان كه مانع حصول مسرت ملاقات شد موجب حسرت خاطر كرديد
٩ انشاء الله تعالے در اثناى راه مقام كانهه پور بزودى ايام از مواصلت صورے
١٠ خورسنديها بحصول خواہد انجاميد و از ملاقات راجه صاحب موصوف
١١ مسرور كشت و حسب الارقام آن مهربان راجه موصوف بدولت
١٢ ملازمت حضور نوابصاحب ممدوح فايز كردانيد و عرضى مرسوله نيز
١٣ از دست شان بحضور كذشته جواب حاصل شده ميرود از ان
١٤ مراتب تفصلات اين سر كار واضح خواہد كرديد ترصد كه مخلص را
١٥ پيوسته خواہان خيريتها انكاشته تا دست داد مواصلت صورے
١٦ بارقام مكاتبت بهجت آيات مسرور و مبتهج مينموده باشند زياده حدّ

Stewart 1825, pl. 21.

Notes

A line is drawn to mark the beginning of the the document. In this example and those that follow, the writing begins below the line, stays close to it, but often rises through it. See Guide no. 1. In **جناب** in line 3, **همركاب** in line 4, and **گرديد** in line 14 it appears that the scribe has stopped to shift the paper and resumed writing at a point that does not require a new penstroke.

Line by line:

1: **سنه** here and in line 2 is a logograph. Almas ‘Ali Khan Bahadur was

Collector General of Oudh.

2: at the end of this line it is easy to make the mistake of reading the extended ی of عیسوی in line 1 as attached to سرور.

4: لارد صاحب refers to Lord Wellesley.

6: here and in lines 8, 10, 12, and 13 in حصول, حضور, and وصول, and also in متضمن in line 2 and نوابصاحب in line 12, the ص has a tall tooth and is joined from below with a deep curve. مهربان here and in line 8 is reduced to two penstrokes. See Guide no. 43.

9: in کانهه پور, ه is written twice to signal that the ه following the ن is aspirated; see also Exx. 49:4, 64:4, 65:3, and 67:4,5.

13: the ر of حضور is missing.

16: for زیاده حدّ see Guide no. 8.

بعز عرض عالی متعالی حضرات ایلچیان خداوند نعمت و کرم معظم حق و مظهر فیض اتم دام ظلال افضاله

میرساند تفصیل نامه نامی السامی الابرار این عقیدت کیش در بهترین روزی یافته قدوم مقصبات

فرط عنایت و معاینت از پیشگاه مکرمت اصدار یافته بود فرق اخلاص و عقیدت را به اوج افتخار و عزت

سود شکرگذاری این چنین عطیه کبری و موهبت عظمی را بکدام زبان ادا نماید خداوند عالم و عالمیان ذات بابرکات

آن خداوندگار را الی یوم التناد سلامت و پاینده داشته فدویان عقیدت شعار را همیشه از اقبال و صولت

آن حضرت عالمیان بهره ور و کامیاب داراد دعای شبانروزی در بقیه زندگانی وظیفه اخلاص‌مندی و عبودیت شعاری نظر

داشته نفسی چند که از حیات ناپایدار باقیست در حسرت مهاجرت و دوری بسر خواهد برد فدوی عقیدت

صبر و شکیبایی شعار چندی است در زاویه خمول و ناکامی بسر میبرد اگر کلمه در حق این خاکسار بجناب والای

لارد و صاحب بهادر ارشاد خواهند شد مدتی روزگار این درمانده بسر حکم اکسیر اعظم خواهد داشت

زیاده ایام خداوندی بپاید ظل فضل و کرم ممدود باد

١ بعز عرض عالے متعالے جناب فیضماب خداوند نعمت و کرم معدن جود و مظہر
فیض اتم دام ظلال افضاله

٢ میرساند تفضل نامه نامی بسرافرازی این عقیدتکیش دیرین و پرورش یافتۀ
قدیم که بمقتضاے

٣ فرط عنایت بیغایت از پیشکاه مکرمت اصداریافته بود فرق اخلاص و عقیدت را به اوج
افتخار و عزت

٤ سود شکر کذاری اینچنین عطیه کبری و موہبت عظمی را بکدام زبان ادا نماید خداوند
عالم و عالمیان ذات با برکات

٥ آن خدایکان را الے یوم التناد سلامت و پاینده داشته فدویان عقیدت شعار را بیمن
اقبال و حکومت

٦ ان فیضرسان عالمیان بہره ور و کامیاب دارد دعای شبانروزی در بقیه زندکانے
وظیفه اخلاصمندی و عبودیت شعارے

٧ داشته نفسی چند که از حیات ناپایدار باقیست در حسرت مہاجرت و دوری بسر
خواہد اورد فدوی عقیدت طراز

٨ صبر و شکیبائی شعار خود ساخته در زاویه خمول و ناکامی بسر میبرد اکر کلمۀ در
حق این خاکسار بجناب والای

٩ لارد صاحب بہادر ارشاد خواہد شد مس روزکار این درمانده را حکم اکسیر اعظم
خواہد داشت

١٠ زیاده حد ادب ندید ظل فضل و کرم ممدود باد

Stewart 1825, pl. 19.

Notes

Characteristic of this hand are long extended final ی and ن, lengthened ـس and ـب-forms, and long diagonals for ک. Examples of را in the shekasta style appear in lines 3, 4, 5, and 9. Final ن is recurved in lines 2 and 8, extended in line 5, and normal elsewhere.

Line by line:

2: the writing begins below the line and ascends to a point well above it at the end. See Guide no. 1, and Ex. 6 for a discussion of this line.

3: for ریا in اصداریافته, see Guide no. 43.

4: for زبا of زبان, see Guide no. 43.

5: the ے of الے is disproportionately small: see also زندگانے in line 6. For ویا of فدویان and نده of پاینده see Guide nos. 43, 72.

6: for the ره of بهره see Guide no. 72. The extended ی of اخلاصمندی interferes with طراز below it in line 7. The superposed ے of شعارے interferes with the dots of the ش.

7: the دو of دوری is a logograph. See Guide no. 7.

9: for the نده of مانده را see Guide no. 72.

10: the simplifaction of باد is easier to understand when it is compared with ارشاد in line 9.

راجع به سینمای اراک — شماره

ساحت صفا حضرت شفیق مهربان گرامی آقای [illegible] مخلصان سلامت

تمنای دریافت نعمت ملاقات و ارفع همه به مرتبه ایست [illegible] خامه

مقطوع اللسان حرفی از دفتر آن در هیچ مرحله قرطاس ثبت نماید

[illegible] تشدید قلم را از آن وادی منصرف خسته ملالت میگرداند

[illegible] اصل بحث شمول بعد استدلال ایام [illegible] عطر

[illegible] ادیب با خلعت فاخره از حضور [illegible] اندر گشته به بلاد [illegible]

با حقایق الفلق و استطلاع کیفیت تعلق [illegible] در آن [illegible] و در حین

انتظار زوال خورمی و خورسندی خاطر گرداند حق [illegible] عطار [illegible]

مبارک و فرخنده گرداند حقایق از صنع [illegible] محمدی [illegible] کمال

[illegible] تعلق خالصه [illegible] بر [illegible] نمونه از دست

مستاجران مجله نوشته گرفته و الفصل [illegible] تعلق تمدید آن را بعنوان

مدیر الامور در [illegible] الایام صدور [illegible] خواهد [illegible] تخصیص آن [illegible] حصول

ملاقات میسر [illegible] حصول [illegible] حقتعالی [illegible]

نیز [illegible]

[illegible]

١ بنام راجه سیتا رام راج

٢ راجه صاحب مشفق مهربان کرمفرمای مخلصان سلامت

٣ تمناي دريافت نعمت ملاقات وافے المسرت به مرتبه است كه بدستیاری خامه

٤ مقطوع اللسان حرفے از دفتر ان درین پرچه قرطاس ثبت مے نماید

٥ لهذا عنان شبدیز قلم را از ان وادی معطوف ساخته بمطلب میکراید

٦ وصول بهجت شمول بعد امتداد ایام نامه عنبرین شمامه متضمن عطاء

٧ زنجیر فیل و اسپ با خلعت فاخره از حضور میستر اندریس به ملازمان انمهربان

٨ با حقایق انضلع و استطلاع کیفیت تعلقه دوستدار در آوان نیك و در حین

٩ انتظار انواع خورمي و خورسندي خاطر کردید حقسبحانه جلشانه عطاء مسطوره

١٠ مبارك و فرخنده کرداناد حقایق اینضلع انفصال جمعبندی سالحال محال

١١ ایچهاپور یا غیره تعلقه خالصه بمبلغ یك لك و شست هزار روپیه نموده از دست

١٢ مستاجران مچلکه نوشته کرفته و انفصال جمعبندي تعلقه زمینداران بعون

١٣ مدیر الامور در معدود الایام صورت انفصال خواهد یافت مخلص اراده مصمم بنابر حصول

١٤ ملاقات میستر اندریس جیو بطرف اسحاق پتن دارد حقتعالے راست آرد

١٥ نیز میخواهد که اکر دولت ملازمت انمهربان چهره افروز بهجت شادکامی کردد

Now turn the page upside down and read from the top down.

١٦ عنوان حصول

١٧ نعمت بقسمے که در خاطر

١٨ بکذرد نوکریز خامه باید ساخت

١٩ چون کارها یکدیکر بمنزله واحد است در صورت اتفاق

٢٠ مراتب اختلاط چنانچه باید تمشیت پذیر خواهد کردید و

٢١ از بند و بست پرکنات و قلاع تعلقه آن مهربان نیز

٢٢ اطلاع دهند ترقب که تا نیل ملاقات بصدور

٢٣ تودد نامجات مسرور مبتهج میداشته باشند زیاده جز

٢٤ شوق چه تصدیع دهد ایام دولت و شادمانے کامرانے باد

٢٥ یازدهم ١١ ماه ١١ شعبان دسنبهر سنه ١٧٦٩ فقط (؟)

Stewart 1825, pl. 15.

Notes

A letter from a British Commissioner. While many letters and words are clearly formed and relatively few dots are missing, there is a lack of consistency in the proportions of the letters. Many of the features already seen are here but in a less regular form, such as the را of راجه in line 1, the چ of پرچه in line 4, and the س of قرطاس in the same line. Final ت, separate or connected, varies between its normal shape (e.g., نعمت in line 3) and an extended and deeply curved version (دریافت in the same line) similar to the ta'liq style. In المسرت in line 3, and آنمهربان in lines 7 and 15, the ا appears to be written as an upward stroke. See discussion in Guide no. 26.

Line by line:

2: رما in کرمفرما is written as a ligature: cf. ملازمان in line 7.

4: the مے near the end is minimized

5: the ل of مطلب is minimized.

6: the final ن of متضمن is extended, the only instance of this in the entire example. The hamza at the end of the line is exaggerated: see also line 9.

9: for the ره of مسطوره see Guide no. 72.

14: جیو: a term of endearment: cf. Pers. جان.

19: the ا of است, which is connected to what follows, is written with a serif.

20: the ه of خواهد is connected to the preceding ا and joins the د from below.

~~پانزدهم ماه جولای ۱۹۰۱ سنه ۱۳۱۹ که در این غنچه جا محفوظ ذخیره~~

رعایای این ممالک ساکن کابل به بر کنه بلیا متصل جبال و کوهستان مردم

سال از قدیم الایام است که در و هند مردمان دستور است بلکه به فقرا

کمی مندرج است در نولایت مذکور از راه کاری و زیادتی کسی سازد فتن

نمیدهد با التقدیر اگر کسی آزار سال بر وه مذکور جمع بدست کفر حکم

غلبه بر سال گیران میکند لهذا رفع این را بد کاری به نام برف سرا

بخصوص طلب التفات نسبت حق فرمایند

پانزدہم ۱۵ ماه جولایے سنه ۱۷۷۵ انکریزي عرضے جان محمد خان و غیره
زین الدین مُلاّ نامے ساکن کاسے پور پرکنه بلیا متصل حویلی دکن نامبُرده
راه از قدیم الایام است امد و شد مردمان و ستورانست بلکه بدفتر
کمپنے مندرج است درینولا ملاّ مذکور از راه شرارت و زبردستے کسے را رفتن
نمیدہد با التقدیر اکر کسے از آن راه برود ملاّ مذکور چوبے بدست کرده حمله و
غلبه بر راه کیران میکند لہذا فدوي امیدوار است که نامبرده را
بحضور طلبیده انصاف حق فرمایند فقط

Stewart 1825, pl. 9, no. 1.

Notes

Many dots are missing and many clusters of dots are reduced to one. Initial ا is usually connected to what follows and is written with a serif in lines 3, 4 (particularly pronounced), and 6.

Line by line:

1: final د following ز in پانزدہم is an open loop. The ہ of ہم is lengthened to accommodate the figure ۱۵.

2: د following ل in الدین descends like ر (see also فدوی in line 6). The zammas over نامبرده ملاّ are exaggerated: compare this with the و at the end of line 5. In every instance in this example ملاّ is written with a tashdid: in this case the tashdid, a zamma, and the dot of the following ن are clustered. Final ن is recurved in دکن، ساکن، الدین; final ل in متصل is shallow and extended. Final ه of نامبرده is incorporated in the incurved tail of د: see also the end of line 6.

3: راه is written similarly in lines 3, 5, 6. The ا of راه is a tall loop and the ه is incorporated in its upcurved tail (in lines 5 and 6 both loops are open). For clear examples of this sort of ا, see را at the end of lines 4 and 6. است is written as a single penstroke: the س and ت are a straight line, lacking teeth, and a final upturn; see also line 4. The ا of آمد lacks a madda. The dots of the ش of شد are clustered into a figure resembling a 9. In مردمان the د is connected to the ر as an open loop with an upturned tail which continues as ما (see also فرمایند in line 7); final ن is superposed.

4: the head of final ج in مندرج is an open loop and suggests a final ع. The ه of راه here is a simple downcurve with a hook under it. The ش of شرارت is a steeply slanted stroke blending smoothly with the following ر: its dots are indicated by a short vertical stroke. The ر of زبردستے is a vertical stroke (see Guide no. 45) and the د is an open loop, as in مردمان in line 3 and برود in line 5. The dot of the ن in رفتن is incorporated in the upcurve (see also آن in line 5). کمپنی: East India Company.

5: The بی of چوبی is minimized and enclosed within the upcurve of the و.

7: In طلبیده the ب and ی are not distinguished, the ی is lengthened, and the د is a simple tooth. The ف of انصاف begins with a short vertical stroke instead of a loop. فقط is a closing formula.

~~بر زمان ماه جوالیه ... الملزنی غرض سلام کلمات کلی ... ~~

بمقام بار ربک پورو منی پور میجر ستیر بارکلی صاحب جمیع سپاهیان در انجا

جهات نمفه ستند در موضع باری جاتیر و غیره تعلقه موکل شیده

سپاهان عبور کنند نمفه لشکریان بار رنجه و باشلی وغیره دفعات رعایای

موضع مذکور بوده و تاراج نموده اذیت میرسانند از ... و

سپاهان سرکار کمپنی انگریز بحکومت ... بعرض میرسانند که

میجر صاحب حکم شود که از بدعتی و تعدی باز داشته رعایای معموره

ایند از رسانند موجب ... بعرض رسانید

١ بیست و نهم ٢٩ ماه جولائے سنه ١١٧٧٥ انگریزی عرضے رام کمار وکیل کشن پرشاد
٢ بمقام باریك پور و منی پور میجر مستر مارگین صاحب جمیع سپاہیان در انجا
٣ چھاونے نموده ہستند در موضع بادی جاتره و غیره تعلقه موکل بنده
٤ سپاہان عبور گنگ نموده اشجارہای انبه و بانس و غیره و خانه ہاے رعایاے
٥ موضع مذکور لوٹ و تاراج نمُوده اذیت میرسانند از بدعت و تعدے
٦ سپاہان تخلل مال کذاری سرکار است بنا بران بعرض میرساند که یکچٹھی بنام
٧ میجر صاحب حکم شود که دست از بدعت و تعدے باز داشته رعایاے موضعمذبور را
٨ ایذا نرسانند واجب بود بعرض رسانید فقط

Stewart 1825, pl. 9, no. 2.

Notes

Certain inconsistencies of writing style appear in this example: نموده is written in the same manner in lines 3 and 4 but differently in line 5. The combination نند is written normally in میرسانند in line 5, but differently in بنده in line 3 and نرسانند in line 8. The combinations ره and ده at the ends of words in lines 3 (twice), 4, and 5 are written with the tail of the ر or د curving around to form the loop of the final ه (see Guide no. 71). Independent final ی is written extended (lines 1, 3, 4, 6), recurved (lines 4, 5, 7), and minimized in a number of other cases. گ appears to be distinguished from ک in lines 2 and 4 by a dot above the diagonal.

Line by line:

1: the ی of بیست is not distinguished. The hamza in جولائی is written as a zig-zag. ١ appears to be repeated in the date. While عرضی is the expected word in this position, because of the dot we cannot rule out the reading غرضی. The letters of رام are written as a single penstroke. Final ل of وکیل is extended.

2: the dot of the ن in مارگین touches the top of the upcurve. The ص of صاحب lacks the tooth following the loop. The م of جمیع appears to be missing. The ن of سپاهیان is extended and superposed (also in lines 4 and 6).

3: the و in چهاونی (a barracks or cantonment) curves up to form the ن and continues on to become a ے within the و.

4: the last three syllables of خانه های are stacked.

5: لوٹ: loot, plunder. The ٹ is an Urdu letter.

6: the first ل of تخلل is very short and the second is extended, as is the ل of مال. The ن of بران is extended and superposed. چٹھی, an Urdu word meaning a letter or chit, is reduced to a logograph and the aspirated ٹ is not distinguished.

7: the dots of the ش of شود are clustered into a figure resembling a 9 (see also Ex. 9, line 3). The ت of بدعت curves deeply downward in a manner often found in this style. موضع and مذکور are run together.

8: for فقط see Ex. 9:7 and Guide no. 8.

غریب پرور سلامت [illegible] دلالی صاحب سکنه مبان [illegible] علاقه ملک [illegible]

بمقدمه زد و کوب کنانیدن لعل محمد سکنه بلی بار [illegible] عدالت

فوجدار ضلع [illegible] بنام فدوی [illegible] صاحب [illegible] فدوی در کوتلی

رانشم [illegible] گردیده بمقام بودن رفته سکونت [illegible] برای احضار

صاحب مرقوم از حضور [illegible] ولد [illegible]

بلکس جرای حضور بنام صاحب [illegible] ضلع [illegible] صاحب [illegible]

زیاده دریں جا [illegible] سوال و جواب [illegible] فدوی [illegible]

فدوی شیخ مولا [illegible]

١ بعد غریب پرور سلامت   مستر ولٹن صاحب ساکن میان بندر متعلقه ضلع مرشداباد

٢ بمقدمه زد و کوب بنالشے لعل محمد ساکن پلٹن بازار بکچهیری عدالت

٣ فوجداری ضلع مرشداباد فدوے را حاضر ضامن داده بے اطلاع فدوی در کوتهی

٤ ریشم نوکر کردیده بمقام پورنیه رفته سکونت میدارد برای احضار

٥ صاحب مرقوم از حضور تقید کردیده   لهذا امیدوارام که قطعه چٹهے معه

٦ یککس چپراسے حضور بنام صاحب جج ضلع پورنیه صادر کردد که صاحبمذکور را
بحضور ارسال

٧ فرمایند که درینجا حاضر کردیده سوال و جواب مقدمه خود پردازد و مخلصے فدوی
شود واجب بود عرض نمود

lower left

٨ عرضے

٩ فدوی شیخ معز الدین

upper left

١٠ حکم شد

١١ که طلب چٹهے بجویاندن پیاده بنام ولٹن صاحب جاری نموده شود

١٢ که پیاده مذکور باطلاع صاحب فوجداری ضلع پورنیه نامبرده را

١٣ کرفتار کرده بحضور ارد بتاریخ ١٢ ماه اپریل سنه ١٧٩٧ انکریزی

upper right

١٤ العبد شیخ معز الدین

Stewart 1825, pl. 11.

Notes

This hand is more consistent than previous ones in forming final ی and ن but less consistent in the size of individual letters; final ن is always recurved in the main text (lines 1, 2, 3, 9). چٹهی is reduced to a logograph. Aspirated consonants in کوتهی and چٹهی (lines 3, 5, 11) are not distinguished. The writing on the upper left of the page is a response to the petition and was written after the main body of text. The writing on the upper right was added last in token of the petitioner's having seen the judgement at the upper left.

Line by line:

1: the شد of مرشداباد is written as a logograph (see also line 3, and شد in line 10).

2: there is an unexplained diagonal stroke above بنالشے. The ل of لعل is shallow and extended. کچیری or کچہری: a provincial administrative office. For notes on the position of the کچہری in the Mughal administrative hierarchy see John R. Richards, *Document Forms for Official Orders of Appointment in the Mughal Empire,* Cambridge, 1986, pp. 62–63.

3: the ا of حاضر is minimized. کوتهی or کوٹهی: a factory.

4: in احضار the ض appears to be repeated.

5: the ه of گردیده continues the upturned tail of the د. امیدوارم is written with an extra ا, as though the enclitic pronoun was a separate word.

6: صادر is written as one penstroke. صاحب and مذکور are run together. The hook on the tail of the ج of جج is the dot of the ب of صاحب. چپراسی: a messenger, orderly.

7: the initial ا of اینجا is elided.

12: نامبرده را is written as three penstrokes.

13: the diagonal stroke following ۱۲ is used to indicate the ordinal number in dates (e.g., 12th; see Guide no. 12). انگریزی is a good example of how commonly-used words can become unreadable to the non-specialist.

اقدس ـــــــ بلد [illegible]

عریضه نوکر [illegible] تاریخ [illegible] ۱۹ ماه [illegible] سال [illegible] ۱۲۰۲ [illegible] روز [illegible] ۲۳ [illegible]

شکر منعم را بجا می آورم متعلق [illegible] [illegible] را با [illegible] فعلاً [illegible] با [illegible]

خواه خود [illegible] روز [illegible] [illegible] طهران گشته است و [illegible]

چهار کس میهمان [illegible] [illegible] واپس [illegible]

[illegible] الحمد لله و [illegible] [illegible] [illegible]

از روی عدالت [illegible] زیاده [illegible]

١ العبد

٢ غریب نواز سلامت بتاریخ نوزدہم ١٩ ماه ساون سنه ١٢٠٣ فصلے روز سه ٣ شنبه
مسمے بهاکت

٣ ساکن موضع داتابهارے متعلقه پرکنه بلیا همشیره منمظهر را باتهام فعل شنیعه با
برادر

٤ خورد خود قریب صبح روز مذکور به ضرب طبر بجان کشته است و کواها اینمعنے

٥ چهار کس مسمیان کوبر دهن و نرائن سنکه و دبو سنکه و اساکوزاست (؟)

٦ موضع مذکور است لهذا امیدوار فضل و کرم است که خونے مذکور را طلبیده

٧ از روی عدالت انصاف فرمایند که بداد خود برسد زیاده حد ادب

٨ عرضی سروپ مدعی — in the left margin

Stewart 1825, pl. 10.

Notes

Line by line:

2: the ه of نوزدهم is lengthened to accommodate the figure 19; فصلی refers to the local agricultural year. ساون: the fourth Hindu month, falling in July–August.

3: من and مظهر are run together. The final ر of برادر is superposed.

4: تبر is spelled with ط. گواه هان lacks its second ه and final ن.

5: there are four personal names, the last of which cannot be deciphered.

6: the sense requires ند after مذکور, but است is clearly written. The ل of فضل is shallow and extended.

7: حد ادب is stacked above زیاده.

8: this line, which includes the signature, appears to be in a different hand.

نقل مطابق اصل العبد

یار علی سررشته دار عدالت دیوانی صدر

تاریخ سی و یکم ماه نومبر ۱۷۹۵ انگریزی [illegible] صدر [illegible] وکلای عدالت حاضر [illegible]

[illegible] کورت و وکلا [illegible] نقل [illegible]

۲

۵۱ نمبر

[illegible]

~~[illegible]~~

[illegible] کورت [illegible] عدالت [illegible]

[illegible] دهم ماه سپتمبر ۱۷۹۵ عیسوی از حضور [illegible] کورت [illegible]

[illegible] عدالت [illegible] صدر [illegible]

[illegible] عدالت [illegible]

حضور صدر [illegible]

Top of the seal:

مهر عدالت دیوانے صدر ۱۲۰۷

To the left of the seal:

۱ نقلمطابقاصلالبعید

۲ یار علی سررشته دار عدالت دیوان صدر

۳ بتاریخ بیست و یکم ماه نومبر سنه ۱۷۹۵ انکریزی سیام سندر پنڈت وکیل عدالت
حاضر آمده قطعه در خواست منظوری اپیل

٤ مع دسمس کورت و وکالتنامه اسمے خود از طرف اپیلانت داخل نمود

۵ نقلش بتفصیل اینکه

٦ ۲ ۵۱ نمبر

۷ (vertically) العبد وکیل عدالت دیوانی صدر سبام سندر پنڈت از طرف کدادہر مہاپاتر

۸ ۱

۹ عادل زمان سلامت

۱۰ کدادہر مہاپاتر ساکن جولے دانکا متعلقه ضلع بشنپور بعرض میرساند فدوی از
دکری ضلع

۱۱ ناراض شده بعدالت کورت اپیل علاقه کلکته حاضر آمده بنام رام کنت مہاپاتر ساکن
نج بشنپور بمبلغ

۱۲ یکہزار سیصد سے و پنجروپیه دوازده آنه نالش نموده بتاریخ دہم ماه سپتمبر سنه
۱۷۹۵ عیسوی از حضور صاحبان کورت مرقوم نالش

۱۳ دادخواه نامسموعه کردیده از انجا نیز ناراض شده بحضور عدالت ظہور صدر حاضر
آمده امیدوار

۱٤ فضل و کرم است که سمن بطلب اسامے و پروانه طلب کاغذات عز اصدار یابد که از
عدالت عالم ارا ے

۱۵ حضور صدر بحق انصاف خود رسیده بدعاے دولت صاحبان عالیشان مشغول و موظف
باشد واجب بود عرض نمود

Stewart 1825, pl. 12.

Notes

A letter to the supreme court of appeals in Calcutta. We have transcribed the page from top to bottom, except for the lines in the seal which are not in the Arabic script. The numerals ۲ and ۱ may have been added later.

Attached final ن is always written extended. Final ی is usually either extended or recurved. Final ه is an exaggerated hook.

The middle two lines on the seal are in Bengali script and the lower two are in *Kaitī*, a script that was in use in eastern Bihar and western Bengal (for an illustration of this script, see Gaurishankar Hirachand Ojha, *The Palæography of India,* 3rd ed., New Delhi: 1971, pl. 78, top).

One of our readers has suggested that the writing of lines 1 and 2 may be intended to resemble Gothic script.

Line by line:

1: سر رشته دار: chief record-keeper and reader of a court. صدر seems to be required by the sense, but both the ص and the د are unusual in form.

3: the ه of آمده (see also the same form in lines 11, 13) is a vertical zig-zag: see Guide no. 72. The upright of the ـط forms in قطعه and منظوری is very short: see also line 14. اپیل: appeal

4: اپیلانت: appellant.

6: ۵۱ is the file number.

10: دکری: decree.

11: the ا of آمده has both a madda and a serif, which is unusual. کورت اپیل: court of appeals.

14: سمن: summons.

15: the ه of رسیده is written separately. In باشد the با runs into the logograph for شد. See Guide no. 48.

مسوده

غره ربیع الاول

فضایل مآب مولوی العهد السعید متوطن قصبه بدبانه محمد آلسمعی که از کثرت عیال و

قلت معاش دلواپس و فکار است که چیزی بوجه ازکار فیض آثار مقرر شود به بابت عیال و حسن

طلباء دیگر معاش کرده در تدریس علم مشغول شده دعاگوی ازدیاد عمر و جاه و وظیفه و ورد حکومت سال

باعث اسم جمیل در دنیا و اجر جزیل در آخرت خواهد شد آفتاب عمر و دولت تابان و درخشان باد

۱ غریب پرور سلامت
۲ فضلیت مآب مولوی احمد سعید متوطن قصبه بدہانه محال آلتمغا سرکار کثرت
عیال و
۳ قلت معاش دارد امیدوار است که چیزی یومیه از سرکار فیض آثار مقرر شود که با
عیال و چندے
٤ طلباء دیکر معاش بسر برده در تدریس علم مشغول شده دعاء ازدیاد عمر و جاه وظیفه
و ورد خود سازد
۵ باعث اسم جمیل در دنیا و اجر جزیل در آخرت خواہد شد آفتاب عمر و دولت تابان و
درخشان باد

Stewart 1825, pl. 13, no. 3.

Notes

Many of the initial and final -س forms are written as almost-vertical strokes (e.g., سعید and سرکار in line 2; معاش and شود in line 3). There is stacking at the end of lines 2–5.

Line by line:

2: the ت of فضلیت curves deeply and resembles those written in the ta'liq style (see also قلت in line 3). The ح of احمد is a loop. محال آلتمغا سرکار: lands granted in perpetuity by the government.

4: final hamzas of طلباء and دعاء are exaggerated and written below the (theoretical) base line. Note the final ه of شده.

5: the ا of دنیا is minimized. شد is written as a logograph.

نواب صاحب جناب مستطاب والا حضرت اجل اکرم افخم ... العدل ... ادام الله اقباله

به عرض | به عز تقدیم محترم می‌رساند که عرض عقیدت عمیقه نمود | می‌رساند

والانامه ملوکانه سرافراز و پرورده پرورانه موزخه ... رسید که ... در جواب عریضه ... شرف ارادت ... و معاودت این بنده احسان

با وضع آسمانی رسید و از احوال جهان ... و ... و الله ... همه آرزو داشتم ما دام حضور ... رضا عالی ... خاص الکمال ... ارسال

ساعی ... عنایت ... از احوال عهد ... ارسال ... الدوام ... الاعلی ... محمد ... مبارکها

و ... الکمال و الاتمام ... ... کاملیکار

به ... مبارک ... آرزو ... ازنقل حاصل

الحناب ... نعمت ... مسرور

معروض ... العباد

۱ نوابصاحب والا جناب خورشید قباب خداوند خدایکان فیاض عصر و الدوران معدن
احسان بے پایان ادام الله دولته و اقباله
۲ بعز عرض بعد تقدیم مراسم بندکے و عقدت که عمده مقاصد است میرساند
۳ والا نامه مملو سرفرازی و پروره پروری مورخه پنجم دسمبر بدستخط کرامت نمط
در جواب عرضداشت دیروز شرف ایراد فرموده تارک مباهات و مفاخرت این پرورده
احسان
٤ باوج اسمان رسانید و انرا حرز جان ساخته وثیقه عزت و آبروے خود و اولاد کردانید
همیشه همین آرزو دارد که مادام الحیات در رضاجوئی عالے وسیله نیکنامی و حصول
لطف خاص انجناب را
۵ ساعے بوده عرایص ضراعت و سپاس کذاری از احوال عقیدت اشتمال ارسال میکرده
باشد اکنون علے الدوام دعاے شبانه روزی همین است که حافظ علے الاطلاق
آنجناب را مع مخدومه مکرمه محترمه دامت برکاتها
٦ و صاحبزادکان والا شان مد الله حیاتهم مصون و محروس در ظل حمایت و حفاظت
خویش بوطن مالوف رسانیده بدیدار اقربا و دوستان و ارچبلد صاحب دام اقباله و
دیکر فرزندان نامدار کامکار
۷ مسرور و شادمان کردند و باز اینملك را از قدوم برکات لزوم انجناب طراوت و
نضارت بخشد از مدتها در دل آرزو داشتم که شبیه مبارک انجناب که از مشق
خاصه
۸ انجناب باشد این پرورده نعمت با جان و دل خود برابر کذارد لیکن ادب باظهار ان
رخصت نمیداد اکر آینده کاهے یاد فرموده باینچنین امتیاز و سرفرازے منظور و
۹ معزز فرمایند مزید افتخار و سربلندی خاکسار خواهد بود زیاده حد ادب دولت و
اقبال بیزوال مدام ملازم و قرین رکاب فیض انتساب باد برب العباد

Stewart 1825, pl. 17.

Notes

In this example most dots are lacking. **ط** and **ظ** sometimes lack their upright. There is considerable stacking of words or parts of words within the lines as well as at the end.

Line by line:

3: ط-forms lack the upright in دستخط and نمط, and in لطف in line 4, حافظ in line 5, and منظور in line 8.

5: the د of دعاے runs into the ع. The initial serif of the ا of آنجناب suggests a ص: see also the second آنجناب in line 7. Compare these with the first آنجناب in line 7 and the first word of line 8.

6: ارچبلد: Archibald.

8: in گاہے the vertical stroke after گا is the hook that identifies the ہ in ہے.

9: the ب of بلندی is not visible.

صدر حسب ... هندو

فدویان [illegible] مصاحب جنوبی [illegible] ما نموده

نموده فی ایام ایجات مرزا کالو عهده [illegible] عبث

[illegible] استمرار [illegible] از روی طلب نمود مدام الوقت [illegible] محال [illegible]

[illegible] و در حضور [illegible] التماس [illegible] سرکار [illegible]

لهذا از فضل و کرم [illegible] حواله [illegible] ارام

حاکم [illegible] خاطر [illegible] التماس و [illegible] سرکار [illegible]

فدویان رعایای [illegible] حضور [illegible]

١ فدويان مالكذارى موضع ساجنپور و سلب بشت ماہه بموجب بند و بست صدر
٢ نموده مى ائيم الحال مرزا كالو عهده دار از راه بدعت
٣ از استمرار بشتماہه افزود طلب نموده مدام الوقت پياده محصل داده
٤ پريشان ميسازد درينصورت سربراه دالے اناس فرمايشات سركار نميشود
٥ لهذا از فضل و كرم اميدوار است كه سربراه موضع مذكور حواله بابو رام كانتو
٦ حكم صادر شود كه بجميع خاطر دالے اناس و مالواجب سركار سربراه بوده باشد
واجب بود عرض نمود
٧ عرضے فدويان رعايان موضع ساجنپور و سلب

Stewart 1825, pl. 14, no. 18.

Notes

Medial and final س-forms, and final ب-forms are lengthened. The ه of راه in lines 2, 4, 5, 6 is connected and turns up. The following are examples of the down-turning final ه: نموده and عهده in line 2; پياده and داده in line 3; بوده in line 6.

Line by line:

2: the ا of الحال connects to the ل at the top. See Guide no. 26.

3: the ه of داده meets the flattened ل of محصل. پياده محصل: a soldier placed over defaulters with authority to compel them to pay their arrears.

4: ڈالى: a basket or present of fruit.

5: the ا of لهذا is connected to the ا of از.

دام اقباله [illegible]

[illegible]

موضوع عمل — بعد از ورود

[illegible]

[illegible]

[illegible]

مارس

[illegible]

[illegible]

[illegible]

١ بندکانعالے نوابصاحب عالیجاه خداوند نعمت و کرم فیاض عالمیان دام اقباله و
حشمتهُ
٢ بموقف عقل بعد اداى
٣ اداب کورنش و تسلیمات که سجیه رضیه نیك پروردكان است میرساند که فدوی
دوازدہم شہر صفر
٤ روانه شده بفضل ایزد متعال و میامن تفضلات انجناب کردون ماب بتاریخ ہفدہم ماه
ربع الاول مع الخير و العافیت داخل
٥ بنارس کشته بدعای دولت ابد مدت مشغول و موظف است تفضلاتے که بمقتضاے
٦ غریب نوازی و پرورده پروری از حضور لامع النور نسبت بحال این ذره بیمقدار مبذول
و مصروف شده اکر ہر موی بدن زبانے کویا
٧ شود سر مو از عہده شکر این موہبت عظمی برون امدن نتواند او تعالے انجناب
عالمیان ماب را با انہمه بیکس نوازی و تفضلات جاویدی دایما
٨ بر وساده دولت و حشمت متمکن داشته بر مفارق جہانیان ظل کستر داراد واجب بود
عرض نمود الہی افتاب دولت و اقبال تابان و درخشان باد

Stewart 1825, pl. 20, no. 16.

Notes

This example has even fewer dots than the previous one. With some exceptions, the ascenders and descenders are emphasized. شده in lines 4 and 6, پرورده in line 6, and وساده in line 8 show examples of the non-connecting final ه assimilated to the form of the connected ه as shown in سجیه رضیه in line 3 and داشته in line 8. The upright ر following a non-connecting letter is seen in پرورده in line 6 (see Guide no. 45).

Line by line:

1: the zamma of حشمته is exaggerated.

3: نمك is a possible alternative reading for نیك.

4: the ل of بفضل does not descend and its bowl is flat and extended: see also

داخل in the same line. بتاريخ and الخير are written as single penstrokes.

5: the ل of مشغول does not ascend, and it closely resembles the ف of موظف.

7: عظمى is written with three penstrokes: the ع and the loop of the ظ; the upright of the ظ; and مى. آن جناب is written with two penstrokes.

8: the ت of دولت (twice in this line) is written almost vertically.

ذوات [illegible] ملکه [illegible] مرسولدر

روز میمنت افروز [illegible] ممالک

[illegible]

خداوند تعالی [illegible] شوکتلو [illegible]

عبد الحميد

١ اداب تسلیمات که طریقه بندکانست بجا اورده بعرض والا میرساند

٢ روز میمنت افروز و شهره که اغاز سال این دیار است او سبحانه بر بندکانحضور و دولتخواہان قرب و دور مبارک

٣ و ہمایون کرداند فدوی که بنده حضور است اداب تصدق ارادت بجا اورده نذر مبارکباد ارسال میدارد امیدوار

٤ خداوند است که از نظر فیض ملازمانحضور کذشته بدرجه پذیرائی مستجاب شود زیاده حد ادب

٥ عرضے عبد العلے

Stewart 1825, pl. 14, no. 17.

Notes

Medial ر, when following a non-connecting letter, ascends rather than descends, as in آورده in lines 1 and 3 (see Guide no. 45) and مبارک in lines 2 and 3. Compare these with ارسال in line 3. Relatively few dots are present. The logograph for که finishes with a downward curve.

Line by line

1: والا appears to have been added later in a different hand.

2: the ر of شهره curves back to form the final ه; see also بنده in line 3. ودولتخواهان is written with one penstroke.

3: the د of بنده descends deeply and resembles a ر.

4: the upright of the ظ of نظر is minimized.

5: the signature appears to be in a different hand from that of the document.

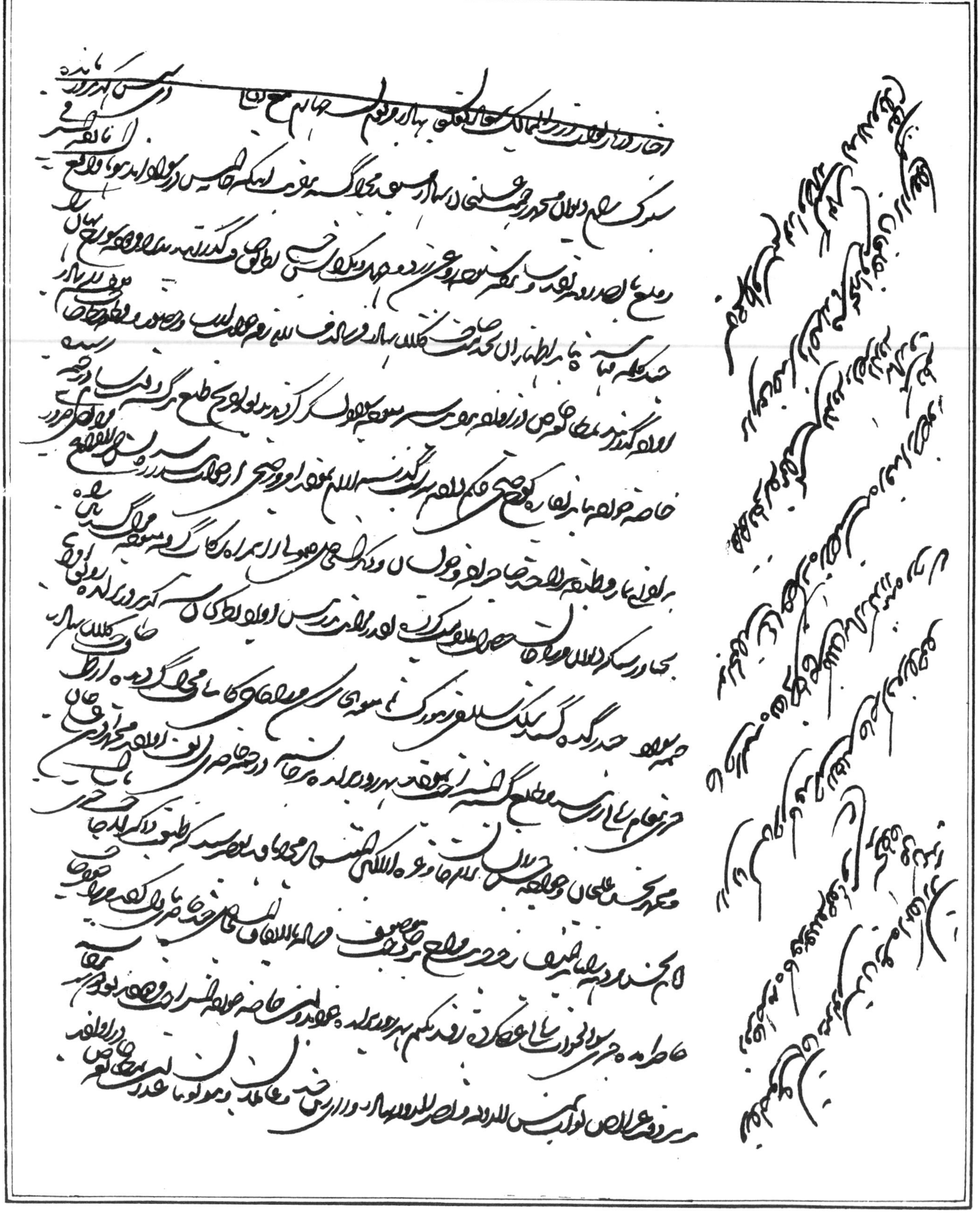

١ اخبار دربار نواب وزیر الممالك سعادتعلیخان بهادر مرقوم است چهارم ربیع الثانی دی شش کهریروز مانده

٢ سیوک رام دیوان محمد رحمت علیخان بهادر مستفید مجرا گشته بتقریب اینکه خانه اش در سواد اندهونا واقع است پانزده اشرفی

٣ و مبلغ پانصد روپیه نقد و شانزده سبوچه روغن زرد و چهل و یکراس خسی بطریق ضیافت گذرانیده پذیرا فرموده سورج بهان را

٤ چند کلمه فهمانیده بنا بر اظهار ان بخدمت صاحب کلان بهادر فرستاد مشار الیه رقعه جواب ادب و حضور و قطعه خط صاحب معظم الیه بهادر

٥ اورده گذرانید بمطالعه خاص در اورده بتقریب سیر متوجه سواد لشکر کردیدند بعد تفریح طبع بر گشته وقت شام در خیمه رسیده

٦ خاصه خورده بنابر اجازه کوچ صبحی حکم داده پهر شب گذشته ارام نموده امروز صبحی از خواب بیدار شده پس از (؟) فراغ فرایض ضروری

٧ به ادای نماز وظیفه پرداختند صاحبزاده و خویشان و دیکر اشخاص معمولی را همراه رکاب گرفته متوجه منزل گشتند بین راه

٨ بهادر سنکه دیوان میرزا جان حصول ملازمت کرده بقدر مراتب نذر پیش اورد نظر کنان سه کهریروز بر امده رونق افزای

٩ خیمه سواد حیدر گده گشتند شلك سلامی زنبورك ها متعینه انجا سر شده مرزا حاجی کامیاب مجرا گردیده از طرف صاحب کلان بهادر

١٠ چیزی پیغام زبانی رسانید مطلع گشته استراحت نمودند پهر روز بر امده بر خاسته در خیمه حاضری تشریف اورده محمد افرین علی خان

١١ و محمد تحسین علیخان و خواجه حسن و انشاء اله خان و غیره اراکین استسعاد مجرا یافتند بعرضرسید که طبعیت داکتر لا صاحب خبری ناساز است

١٢ امام بخش مروهه را (؟) بنابر استفسار خبر خیریت مزاج نزد صاحب موصوف فرستاده بالاتفاق اشخاصی چند حاضری تناول کردید مرزا جعفر خان

١٣ حاضر امده چیزی سوالجواب زبانی عرضکرده رفتند یکنیم پهر روز بر امده خود بدولت خاصه خورده استراحت فرمودند بعد دو پهر برخاسته

١٤ بر سر دفتر عرایض نواب یمین الدوله و نصر الدوله بهادر و رای رتن چند و عاملان و مولویان عدالت بمطالعه خاص در اوردند

Now turn the page upside down and read from top down.

١٥ مرزا اصغر علے خان و مولوی سدن و غیره اہلکاران
١٦ دفتر حاضر امده کاغذ علاقه خودہا مزین بدستخط خاص کنانیدند
١٧ رای دیاکشن چیزی کاغذ حسب الطلب حاضر کرد مرزا جواد
١٨ صاحب رسیده لفافه خطی صاحب کلان بہادر کذرانیده و چیزے
١٩ سوالجواب زبانے عرض کرده رخصت شده رفتند از حضور
٢٠ دو دو قطعه نموده بنواب یمین الدوله و نصر الدوله بہادر و یك قطعه
٢١ برای رتن چند شرف اصدار یافت بمحمد افرین علیخان برای روانکی
٢٢ پیش خیمه طرف سلیم پور امر صادر گشت بعمل امد الا فردا مقام است

Stewart 1825, pl. 24.

Notes

A daily report from the court of Nawab Sa'adat 'Ali Khan Bahadur of Oudh, from 1810. In many cases گ is distinguished from ک. Final ن is often written in an open, extended form, above the line, as in سعادتعلیخان in line 1.

Line by line:

1: گھڑی: the space of twenty-two and a half minutes.

3: خسی for خصی ?

4: صاحب کلان بہادر refers to the British Resident.

6: پہر: a division of time consisting of eight گھڑی or three hours: an eighth part of a day.

8: the reading بہادر is not certain.

9: آنجا is written as one penstroke.

11: the ر of اراکین is a vertical stroke.

12: the reading مرویه is not certain.

17: the upright of the ط of طلب is minimized.

۱

هو الله تعالی

جناب والامناصب معظم و مکرم الطاف فرمای مهربان دام اقباله

سابق از این عریضه‌ای که بخدمت عالی معروض داشته که حکم سرکار اعلی در رسیدن نانها به حضور رسید لطف ... روشن

در ... است ملاحظه ... فرصت ... کل فرموده‌اند که ... حق نواب ... فرصت ... درگاه

سالهاست با کمال ... در کارهای ... و ملک مصروف است باید ... دوری

... فرمایند ... جمع و کفایت ... ویرانه ... حال ملک

از ... رفع ... کفایت ... جمع نمانده است امید که

از صدور ... شوند

ایام دولت و اقبال ... دوران ... باد

١ ہو الفیاض

٢ صاحب والا مناقب معظم و مکرم الطاف فرماے بیکران دام اقبالهُ

٣ سابق ازین عریضه نیاز که بخدمت عالے مرسول داشته ہمکے احوال کثیر الاختلال و
زیرباری تباہے بر ضمیر خورشید نظیر روشن

٤ و ہویداست انچه لازمه فیضرسانے بود ان کرم فرماے فرمودند حق تعالے ان
فیضرسان را تا دیرکاه

٥ سلامت با کرامت داراد که بکار پردازی غریبان و بیکسان مصروف آید امید که نوعی

٦ توجہه فرمایند که حق بحقدار فائز شود و عُسرت خرج و تکلیف ہر کونه که درین
ویرانه بنده حال میکذرد

٧ از توجہه عالے رفع کردد زیراکه الحال (؟) برداشت تکلیفات و تصدیعات خرج
نمانده است امید که

٨ از صدور جواب عرضے سر افرازیہا میفرموده باشد که از ان تسلے تمام و اطمینان ما
لاکلام خواہد شد

٩ افتاب دولت و اقبال تابان و درخشان باد زیاده فقط

Stewart 1825, pl. 18.

Notes

The vertical line at the top of the page has been read by some as a stylized version of باسمه.

Line by line:

2: the zamma of اقباله is exaggerated.

4: the ا of هویدا and the serif of the ا of است appear to be continuous, but this must be accidental, since the former would normally be written with a downstroke and the latter with an upstroke (cf. Guide no. 26). For لازمه cf. Guide no. 45.

5: the final د of داراد is exaggerated.

6: توجه ends with ه written twice to show that the final ه is pronounced. The long downward stroke of the ج results from the scribe lifting the pen off the paper at a point where that was not necessary. Cf. the same word just below in line 7.

8: میفرموده is written as one penstroke.

9: for زیاده فقط see Guide nos. 8, 43.

بعرض بندگان عالی متعالی دام اقباله میرساند به ملاحظهٔ رسیمان و دلیل زرای دهو بقعه

سالکی موضع دارا بهار بمقدر حمل قدری مسعه حمله موضع مذکور رسیده صلوات

حال حمل مذکور بکوابی سالکان موضع مسطور و بمهر حوف و محرر نمایه در سنه بمهر مطلق

عرض بنده ارکان حکم و داشت الی سایه بهابار بر مقارق ما قدویان تحقیق است

پیشانی تا قیام جور بن لب آن خورشید تابان دور خشان باد

عرض بنده محمد ابو حسینی

١ بعرض بندکان عالے متعالے دام اقبالهٗ میرساند به اظهار مسمیان دولال رای و
بودہو راے
٢ ساکن موضع داتابہاری بمقدمه خون فدوی معه عجله بموضع مذکور رسیده صورت
٣ حال خون مذکور بکواہی ساکنان موضع مسطور و بمہر خود و محرر تہانه درست
نموده بملفوف
٤ عرضی ہذا ارسال حضور داشت الہے سایه ہماپایه بر مفارق ما فدویان عقیدت
٥ بنیان تا قیام دوران بسان خورشید تابان و درخشان باد
٦ عرضی فدوے عبد العلے حسینے

Stewart 1825, pl. 10.

Notes

Final attached ی is written extended in lines 3 and 4 and recurved in lines 1, 4, and 6.

Line by line:

1: The لے of عالے and متعالے are superposed. The zamma over the final ه of اقباله is exaggerated. In بودہو it is unusual for the first syllable to be stacked above the second.

2: The reading عجله is not entirely satisfactory. The م of مذکور lacks its eyelet (see also the same word in line 3). مقدمه: case, complaint.

3: تہانه: police station.

6: the dot of the ف of فدوے is far removed.

الملک سپه سالار ... حسین ... نظام الدوله

۱۲۹۰ ... [illegible]

مطالعه صاحب سپه سالار مهربان ... دوستان ... صاحب سلمه الله تعالی

مصحوب یار

صاحب سپه سالار مهربان مخلصا ... سلامت باشید

بعد ... ملاقات ... آن ... مکتوب ... خاطر ... نمودید ...

در ... تعلیم ... نوید ... و ... صاحب ...

در که ... مقام ... ملاحظه ...

[illegible]

صاحب سپه سالار مهربان مخلصا ... صاحب سلمه الله تعالی ...

[illegible]

[illegible]

[illegible]

[illegible]

[illegible]

[illegible]

[illegible]

(The seal)

نصیر الملك انتظام الدوله سید علی خان نصرت جنك بهادر ۱۲۰۰

۱ بمطالعه صاحب بسیار مهربان استظهار دوستان مستر چارلس استورایت صاحب سلمه الله تعالے موصول باد

۲ ۲٤ ماه مارچ سنه ۱۷۹۰ (Vertically in the left margin)

۳ صاحب بسیار مهربان استظهار مخلصان سلامت

٤ بعد شرح اشتیاق ملاقات بهجت آیات که متجاوز التحریر است مکشوف خاطر مهربانے مظاهر نموده مے آید

۵ دیر است که بعدم دریافت نوید خیریت و عافیت و تشریف داشتن آنصاحب مهربان

٦ در کدام مقام دل اتحاد منزل متعلق بود و اکثر اوقات از صاحبان دوستان بمقتضای محبت و ارتباط

۷ استفسار اخبار اخیار مسرت آثار انصاحب مهربان میبود الحمد لله که درینولا از تقریر

۸ صاحب بسیار مهربان مخلصان کپتان مارکن صاحب سلمه اله تعالے که از دوستدار محبت و یکجهتی

۹ بدرجه اتم دارد معلوم شد که آنصاحب مهربان بکانهه پور بخیریت تشریف دارند

۱۰ و شادے کتخداے انصاحب مهربان بمیمنت و فرخی بوجه احسن انجام یافته و کار سرداری فوج

۱۱ که مقدمه ترقیات مدارج است بانصاحب تعلق پذیرفته اینمعنے موجب سرور

۱۲ موفور مخلص مهجور کشته (بیت) ببالید از بسکه بر خویشتن ز شادے

۱۳ نگنجید در پیرهن حقسبحانه تعالے شادے میمنت مبادی را بهزاران عیش و طرب

۱٤ بآنصاحب مهربان مبارک و مهنا سازد و یوماً فیوماً بدرجه اعلے رساند

Now turn the page upside down and read from top to bottom.

۱۵ که نشاط

۱٦ و انبساط دوستان همیشه ازدیاد

۱۷ در ان متصور است از دوستے و مهربانے

۱۸ انصاحب مهربان بسیار تعجب دست داد که در مدت مدید از نامه و پیام

۱۹ خیریت التیام و بشارت تهنیت اشارت حسن انجام شادے و فایز کردیدن بکار

سردارے
٢٠ فوج مسرت افزاے خاطر دوستدار نکردند و دل را که خواہان چنین مژده طرب
پیرای دلہای دوستان است
٢١ اصلا باطلاع ان مسرور نساختند ظہور اینمراتب بعید از مراسم وداد و یکجہتے ہا
است ترصد که دوستدار را
٢٢ بیاد حسن اخلاق رطب اللسان و عذب البیان انکاشته بخلاف اسلاف تا دست داد لقاے
٢٣ بہجت افزا کاه کاه بمراسلات تودد ایات مشعر صحاح مزاج کثیر الابتہاج مسرور و
منبسط
٢٤ میساخته باشند
٢٥ زیاده چه بر طرازد ایام مسرت بکام باد والسلام

Stewart 1825, pl. 16.

Notes

A letter from Nawab Nusrat Jang Bahadur to Charles Stewart. This hand shows some features of shekasta ta'liq, notably the deep final ن which is almost closed at the top, the tall initial ا with a long serif (see Guide no. 25), and final س the bowl of which is almost closed. Many dots are lacking. The arrangement of words on the seal does not correspond to the order of terms in the name.

Line by line:

1: دوستان, here and in all other occurrences, begins with the logograph for دو.

2: the date appears to be in a different hand from the remainder of the text.

4: the ا of آید has both a madda and a serif.

5: the د of دریافت is exaggerated.

12: the symbol after گشته indicates that a line of verse follows: we have added the word بیت.

25: for the ر of طرازد see Guide no. 45. The phrase والسلام is in a larger, heavier script and appears to have been added later.

سواد مکتوبی که بسلطان داراشکوه در جواب آنکه امیر الامرا فرستاده بود

نوباوه حدیقه عظمی و اقبال و نورسته ریاض رنگین دولت و دولت جاوید که استیناف تعلیق

و سر جوش میخانه بهجت و وفا آن گرامی مکتوب بدایع اسلوب فلان در ساعت

مسعود در ساعت محمود رسید که کام محبوبی ابدایه کامروا برآمد آمال ساعت حصول

در ساعت فیض ورزد وارد راند و ذائقه نشاط را ... بس دلگشای جلوه نمایشگاه را

دلکشی ... و لیکن ... رسیدن آن ... بخش ... بهم ...

بجوالی حالت ... هندوستان هواخواه دماغ ... را بالا ... زبان

افزاید از مکتوب بشارت ... در ضمن صحبت ... مکتوب ...

از ... ادوار ... احوال ... هندوستان ... گمان

زبان ... خامه فصیح اللسان ... در مرآت ضمیر ... عیان ...

١ سواد مكتوبے كه بسلطان دارا شكوه ...
٢ نوباوهٔ حديقه دُوستى و اتحاد و ثمر پيش رس يكتادلے و وداد رحيق خمكدهٔ ايتلاف و
ايفاق
٣ و سرجُوش ميخانه مودت و وفاق اعنى كرامى مكتوب بدايع اسلوب فلان در ساعتى
٤ مسعُود و زمانے محمود كه شاہد كامجوئى را پيرايهٔ تمامى (؟) در بر و ساقے آمال را
بادهٔ وصُول و حصُول
٥ در ساغر بود فيض ورود ارزانے داشته ذائقه نشاط و انبساط را شيرين و محفل خلد
مشاكل شيفتكے را
٦ رنكين كردانيد و كيفيت بادهٔ رسيده رسيدن آن زينت بخش دہيم و كاه
٧ بحوالے ممالك بيكران دُوستان ہواخواه دماغ انتعاش را كه بالا رسانيد ازان
٨ افزايد از مكتوب شادى دوستداران را كه فيض صُحبت ياران بود مكتوب
ياران را انچه
٩ از تقاليب ادوار و ازمان و شُورش احوال و اوضاع ہندوستان و نيرنكے چرخ كردان
١٠ زبان زد خامه فصيح البيان شده بود در مرآت ضمير ولا جلوه عيان نمود

Stewart 1825, pl. 22.

The beginning of a draft of a letter from Shah ‘Abbas II to Dara Shukuh. Stewart’s note (p. 174) says: "This letter is taken from a thick volume of the correspondence of Shah Abbas II.; it is written in the Shafia hand ... dated A.H. 1204, (A.D. 1790) and was brought from Persia by the late Major Campbell."

Notes

Line by line:

1: this line appears to be in a different hand from the rest of the letter. The reading of everything after **شكوه** is uncertain. It is instructive to examine some of the reasons for the difficulties with these words. An initial assumption could be that this line was written by a file clerk or an owner of the document to identify and file it. The greatest handicap for the reader is that there is only a very small sample of the script available to facilitate the comparison of letters and combinations, making it difficult to be sure about ambiguous forms. The first two letters after شکوه could be در. The letter above the د could be خ, ص, or possibly ا with a serif, although no other ا with a serif appears in the line. This may be followed by a ب–form and an extended ی or ن. What follows could be the logograph for که, or possibly the figure ۱۸. If it is the former, the next word could be آزاده (although the dot for the ز is rather far to the left); if the latter, it could be the name of a month, a location where the document was kept, or some other noun. The next word could be ایران with the medial ا connected to the ن, but no closely similar combination is found. Next could possibly be متن with a recurved ن, باشد with the logograph for شد, or something else. The final word could be read as برده, or (less likely) نموده, or a word where the final letter curves back to form the dots of a previous letter. Any or all of these readings could be incorrect.

4: the reading تمامی is not satisfactory.

5: there is an unexplained dot over the ر of ورود.

6: آن has both a madda and a serif.

7: the final ک of ممالك is marked by a small ک.

8: the verse has been set off by spaces.

تقریظ حکیم ملک الشعرا

سپاس ربّ قادر کریم را که این ثمره اتفاق و محبت گستری احباب نوع

بعون عنایت کردگار بظهور رسید [illegible] بنده که بالجمله در تطلب

نیک اصحاب مستر و یوسف حضرت حاجی ملا عبدالله آنان باشیم و بکنیم غنیمت

زمان را در المقام حرف کلمه تاریخ [illegible] نمی‌شد

دیگر هزار بار بهشت قهقهه قابل تحریر نیست [illegible]

١ قبله و کعبه بنده دام ظلهٗ
٢ سپاس است قادر کریم را که انچه ثمرهٔ اشفاق و محبت کشی انجناب بود
٣ بعون عنایت کردکار بظهور رسید چون رفتن بنده تا کچهری حسب الطلب جناب
٤ فیضمآب مستر دیوس صاحب دام دولتهٗ اتفاق شده و یکنیم ساعت
٥ زمانے را در انمقام صرف کرده باز عود بخانه نموده شد
٦ دیکر مراتب بجز مشافهه قابل تحریر نیست زیاده عرض چه . . .

Stewart 1825, pl. 13, no. 4.

Notes

Final ه is written in three ways: compare ظله in line 1, and بنده in lines 1 and 3 with شده in line 4, and کرده and نموده in line 5.

Line by line:

1: The ل of قبله scarcely ascends, and the final ه descends deeply. بنده is written as a single penstroke. The tail of the م of دام is recurved. The zamma of ظلهٗ is exaggerated (see also line 4).

3: چون is written vertically and the ن is very extended; contrast this with the ن of رفتن. The ن of جناب is not visible.

4: صاحب, and the دو of دولته, are reduced to logographs.

5: کرده and نموده are each written as a single penstroke.

6: the ی of دیکر is not visible, although its dots are present. The writing after عرض suggests a formula such as چه نویسد but the reading is unclear.

سلمه
علیحضرتا

صاحب عالیقدر مشفق بس مهربان کرم‌های قدردان

بعد از کشتن سواحل معروض میدارد که از یاد ایام ادراک حضور

مشغول خاطر توجه مطالب که بعد مرحوم کلکته دارالانشاء

برای این مشغول اللهم مدد الهی و امداد ارشاد

از لطف و مهربانی‌های دارالسلطنه مذکور به مسطور فرموده

محض سلامت سرور مشغول و خواهد بود و دید

ملاحظه مدرسه‌ای از جلوگیری جمع

مهمان‌ها ایام سرور مطلبی مسند باشد

زیاده ایام بمحبت سامی مستدام ملکم باد

١ صاحب عاليقدر مشفق بسيار مهربان کرم فرمای قدردان مخلصان سلامت
٢ بعد شرح اشتياق مواصلت موفور المسرت که زياده از ان در حد حصر است
٣ مشهود خاطر توجهه مظاهر کردانيده می آيد بيست پنج دالے انبه
٤ برای ان مشفق ابلاغ ميدارد اميد که از راه
٥ اشفاق مهربانے دالے ہا مذکور را منظور فرموده
٦ مخلص را مسرور ممنون فرمايند تا دست داد
٧ ملاقات مسرت سمات از چکونکی مزاج
٨ مهربانے امتزاج مسرور مطمئن ميشده باشد
٩ زياده ايام بهجت شادمانے مدام بکام باد

Stewart 1825, pl. 20, no. 11.

Notes

This text has the fewest dots of any of our examples; most of these dots distinguish ش from س. In addition to a lack of dots, many examples of م are not visible. Final ح-forms look like final ع. که is written in different styles in lines 2 and 4. This sort of hand indicates clearly how readers must depend on recognizing shapes and logographs, as well as be familiar with the verbal formulae of polite prose that different contexts require.

Line by line:

2: the ا of اشتياق has a curved top and the serif is of the same weight as the ا. The ا of است resembles a small ل.

3: ه is written twice at the end of توجه to indicate that the final consonant is pronounced.

4: the ه of راه is an irregular blob.

5: a ی marking the اضافه would be expected following دالے ہا. The ه of فرموده descends deeply.

III

Section III comprises ten official documents from the Qajar period, divided into two sub-sections. The first five are from the mid-nineteenth century (1851-53), and the second five are from the late nineteenth and early twentieth centuries.

Examples in this section come from Vahed-e Nashr-e Asnad 1369 and Safa'i 1346.

۸

بندگان ... ها در ایامی که نوشته‌اید در مهمانی درویش پاشا

شهرت طالع شد سفارت‌های ... در زمان درویش پاشا ... بجهت

دعوت نموده است این شهرت روز بروز تواتر بهم رسانید مخلص گذارش نماید

بوکلای دولت اظهار نمود که آمدن او در چنین وقت لزوم ندارد و

باعث آشوب اهالی سرحد میشود البته بدرویش پاشا خبر بنویسند

آمدن او را موقوف کند سخت و صریح نوشتند آن پهلوان

سفیه ما اعتنائی بآن نوشته نکرد جواب غریب نوشت

و دلخواه خود را بعمل آورد وکلای دولت برای ساکت ... مخلص

و ... خودشان این مضمون را در زبان ساخته‌اند که درویش پاشا

هر قدر زیادتر فساد آشکار نماید وجوهات بی‌حلاف ... اوپانه

قلمی نمایند آنقدر نفع دولت ایران خواهد شد چنین نیست

که اولیای دولت روس و انگلیس اینگونه حرکات خلاف

و ناملایم ... سرحدی شاهنشاهی ... آنکه ... ازین قبیل رفتار باشند

درویش پاشا دلخور شوند و غصه خورند باید همه خوشحال و ... سازند

تا این طایفه عرض ندارم ۱۵ شوال ۱۲۹[illegible] در تحریر ... مخلص

۱ هو
۲ بندکان پناها   در لاهیجان و اشنویه آدمهای درویش پاشا
۳ شهرت داده بودند که پاشای رواندوزرا درویش پاشا بملاقات خود
٤ دعوت نموده است این شهرت روز بروز تواتر بهم رسانید مخلص کزارش را
۵ بوکلای واسطه اظهار نمود که آمدن او در چنین وقت لزوم ندارد
٦ باعث آشوب اهل سرحدّ میشود البتّه بدرویش پاشا چیزی بنویسید
۷ آمدن اورا موقوف کنید سخت و صریح نوشتند ان پهلوان
۸ مفسد ها اعتنائے بآن نوشته نکرد جواب غریب نوشت
۹ و دلخواه خودرا بعمل آورد وکلای واسطه برای تسلے مخلص
۱۰ و دل خودشان این مضمون را ورد زبان ساخته اند که درویش پاشا
۱۱ هر قدر زیادتر فساد آشکارا نماید و جوابهای خلاف و بے ادبانه
۱۲ قلمی نماید آنقدر نفع دولت ایران خواهد شد چنین نیست
۱۳ که اولیای دولت روس و انکلیس اینکونه حرکات خلاف
١٤ و نا لایق را سهل شمارند عوض اینکه شما ازین قسم رفتارهای
۱۵ درویش پاشا دلخور شوید و غصه خورید باید همیشه خوشحال و دل شاد باشید
۱٦ زیاده طاقت عرض ندارم ۱۵ شوال ۱۲٦۸ در مرکور (؟) معروض کردید امر ها مطاع

Vahed-e Nashr-e Asnad 1369 I, p. 594.

Notes

A letter from Mirza Ja'far Khan Moshir al-Dowla to the foreign ministry. Final ل tends to be flattened.

Line by line:

11: the ید of نماید is reduced to a diagonal stroke: see also line 12.

16: the figure for the year was apparently added later and is bracketed by small marks (not represented in the transcription). Only the bottom part of the ع of مطاع is visible, and it curves far back under the ها of امرها.

بوزرای مختار دولتین واسطه نوشته شود

مراسله انگلیسیان متعلق بقضایای سرحدات که بحضور مبارک همایون در آید بهتر باشد بحکم سلطانی از ایران

قوسون مورخه دویم شهر جمادی الاولی رسید و از مطالب مندرجه در آن آگاهی حاصل آمد همان مراسله نزد

بنظر انور همایون اعلیحضرت شاهی روحی فداه رسید چون حکم صریح بجواب نوشتن

و به خیال ادای اندولیت در این باب باکمال اطمینان و رسانی داده بود داده شده

جواب مسوده سابق برای انجامها

محتاج بتفصیل مجدد نیست انجامها را رفت ۲

۱۲۶۹

ملاحظه احترام با شهر جمادی الاولی ۲۳

١ بوزرای مختار دولتین واسطه نوشته میشود صحیح است ثبت شد
٢ مراسله انجنابان متعلق بفقره نهضت موکب همایون در بهار آینده بچمن سلطانیه از
برای سان
٣ قشون مورخه دویم شهر جمدی الاولے رسید و از مطالب مندرجه در ان اکاہی حاصل
آمد ہمان مراسله مزبوره
٤ بنظر انور ہمایون اعلیحضرت شاہنشاہی روحی فداه رسید چون حکم جدیدی بجز بے
غرضی
٥ و بے خیالے اولیای ایندولت در این باب با کمال اطمینانات که سابق داده شد
نفرمودند
٦ و محتاج بتفصیل مجدد نبود که انجنابان را زحمت دہد جواب مفصل ہم سابق بر این
بانجنابان داده شده بود لہذا در جواب مراسله انجنابان
٧ و بابت ملاحظه احترام باین چند کلمه مصدع شد فے ٣ شہر جمدی الاولے ١٢٦٩

Vahed–e Nashr–e Asnad 1369 I, p. 603.

Notes

Dots are often clustered: see, e.g., مختار in line 1.

Line by line:

1: the writing in the upper left corner was added later in a different hand.

6: the large mark above دہد indicates the insertion of the phrase stacked above. Something has been crossed out following مفصل. بانجنابان in the inserted phrase is written with two penstrokes.

جنابا مراسله مورخه هفتم شهر صفر آنجناب در دو باب حکایات تازه سرحدداران

دولت روم به دوستداران نگارش رفته بود رسید شکایات اولیای این دولت را به دولتهای خود

و ایلچیان متوسطین مقیم اسلامبول البته اطلاع خواهند داد و البته گمان دارند در این اظهارات

در دولت ایران شده است خالی از اغراق نباشد زیرا در خصوص اینکه آورده است

دو رأی تازگی میگویند در قطور ظاهر شده است کارگزاران دولت علیه و واسطه در تبریز

هیچ اظهاری در آن باب نکرده‌اند هر چند از مأموران و وکلای دول فرنگ در این باب مذاکراتی در میان دو دولت است

در طایفه عثمانیه جاف را از صرافت تصرف مراعی طایفه کردان ایران منع از دولت

دوستداران بر حسب اللازم سپرده‌اند در ضیقه را بخصوص نمایندگان و وکلای واسطه بیان ورزند البته اطلاع هم

بعد از مسعودی به اقدام در رفع تصرفات والی در هنوز سرحد آن ولایت را وکلای چهار دولت

مشخص نکرده و نقشه برنداشته و ملاحظه نکرده‌اند خواهند کرد و هو الله الباقی بعد الاظهار داشت

تحریر ۱۳ [illegible] ۱۲۶۸

١ جنابا   مراسلهٔ مُورّخهٔ هفتم شهر صفر انجناب که در باب حرکات تازهٔ سرحدداران
٢ دولت روم بدوستداران نکارش رفته بود رسید   شکایات اولیای ایندولت را بدولتهای خود
٣ و ایلچیان مُتوسطین مُقیم اسلامبول البته اطّلاع خواهند داد   و امّید کلّے دارند که این اظهارات
٤ که بدولت ایران شده است خالے از اغراق نباشد زیرا که در خصوص این تجاوزات
٥ که در این تازکے میکویند در قطور ظاهر شده است کارکزاران دولتین واسطه در تبریز
٦ هیچ اظهاری در آن باب نکرده اند   هر چند از بودن وُکلاء در خاک ذهاب بدلیل نزدیك است
٧ که طایفهٔ عُثمانیه جاف را از صرافت تصرّف مراعی طایفهٔ کوران ایران بیندازند ولے
٨ دوستداران بر خود لازم میدانند که اینفقره را بخصوص بخاطر وُکلای واسطه بیاورند البته انها هم
٩ بقدر مقدور اقدام در منع تصرّفات ولایتی که هنوز سرحدّ آن ولایت را وُکلای چهار دولت
١٠ مُشخص نکرده و نقشه بر نداشته و ملاحظه نکرده اند خواهند کرد چونلازم بود اظهار داشت
١١ تحریر ١٢ شهر صفر سنه ١٢٦٨

Vahed-e Nashr-e Asnad 1369 I, p. 579.

Notes

The conventional mark for a change of topic appears in lines 2, 3, and 6: see Guide no. 2. Final ن generally resembles a ل with the bowl curving inward to form the dot.

Line by line:

1: there are kasras under the three hamzas: see also line 6.

6: the ک of خاک has a hamza written above it and a redundant kasra.

در این ایام بقای دولتین علیتین مابین دینیه جامعه جهت از رشته روابط و داد و ربط اتحاد مقتضی

ایران مستقر است [illegible] مخالفت از [illegible] شده [illegible] بنای [illegible] است [illegible] و منتظم

با اتصال [illegible] در حدود ممالک طرفین [illegible] در [illegible]

واقع شود [illegible] مامورین دولتین [illegible] است [illegible]

[illegible] و [illegible] اهالی [illegible] رضای [illegible]

مامورین [illegible] از جانب مامورین دولت [illegible] اجرای آن [illegible] شده [illegible]

مامورین دولتین [illegible] در باب [illegible] اقدام دولت علیه [illegible]

از [illegible] حالی [illegible] مراتب [illegible] مسائل ارجاع

مامورین دولت ایران [illegible] از [illegible] اهالی [illegible] شده از طرف

مسموع [illegible] ملاحظه [illegible] آمده

در [illegible] و اجرای [illegible] محرر [illegible] و اجرا [illegible] در ضمن [illegible] نامه

در بعضی [illegible] حضرت [illegible] جناب [illegible] افندی [illegible] مامور [illegible]

در خصوص [illegible] افندی [illegible] آن از طرف [illegible]

[illegible] اظهار [illegible] کارگزاری [illegible] آن [illegible]

[illegible]

١ هو

٢ باقتضای اتحاد و رابطه وداد که با رشته زرتار جهت جامعه دینیه مابین دولت علیّه ابدی القیام و دولت بهیه

٣ ایران منعقد و مستحکم است همیشه تحکیم مبانی مخادنت و تشیید ارکان مخالصت را مستلزم است

٤ با استحصال وسایل مرغوبه در حدود ممالك طرفین تطاول و دست درازی که مغایر عهد و مصافاتست

٥ واقع نشود و بر ذمت مصادقت مامورین دولتین فخیمتین مرتب است که مثل این حالات غیر مرضیه وقوع نیابد

٦ سنجاق ذهاب که داخل ایالت بغداد بود پیش از این مبنی بهر سببی بوده بخلاف رضای شاهی و منافے شروط

٧ معاهدت بتقریبی از جانب مامورین دولت ایران باخذ آن متحاسرت شده بمراعات لازمه موالاة

٨ که مابین دولتین علیتین بر قرار است در باب اینکه سنجق مزبور کما فے القدیم بدولت علیه واکذار شود چیزی

٩ از اینمقوله تا حال کفتکو نشده همین طور مانده مع هذا بملاحظه مراتب مزبوره و اقتضای مسالمت از جانب

١٠ مامورین دولت ایران بنابر اینکه سنجق مذکور از مضافات ایالت بغداد بوده کف ید از آنجا شده از طرف

١١ مستجمع المجد و الشرف شاهنشاه والا جاه نیز در این باب بملاحظه استقرار مخادنت کامله لازم آمده

١٢ که بر (؟) طبق ایجاب و اجرای حالات مخدومه اظهار موافقت و اجرا فرمایند دیکر در ضمن اخلاص نامه

١٣ که در بعضی خصوص خیریت تمهید و بیان شده عزت پناه کمال افندی بدانصوب مامور و عازم بود

١٤ در خصوص مذکوره نیز بافندی مومی الیه اشعار آن مناسب مینمود کیفیت آن از طرف اشرف بسوی والا

١٥ اشعار و اظهار شد اقتضای شیمه کارکزاری و فتوه دائیه عالے آن است که لوای مزبوره کما فے السابق

In the right margin:

١٦ بطرف دولت علیه رود تسلیم حضرت
١٧ والـے بغداد شود در اینباب بتمنای اینکه
١٨ همم علیه در اجرای این کار مصروف
١٩ فرمایند بخصوصه این وداد نامه تحریر و
٢٠ همراه افندی مومی الیه ارسال شد
٢١ انشاء اله تعالـے لدی شرف الوصول بر وجه
٢٢ متمنا همم بهیهٔ مصروف فرموده
٢٣ منوط شیمه فتوت شعارشان است

Vahed-e Nashr-e Asnad 1369 I, p. 533.

Notes

Final ت is sometimes in the ta'liq style. Many examples of final ن are recurved.

Line by line:

11: لازم is a series of vertical strokes of about the same height. See Guide no. 45.

13: the ز of عزت suggests a medial ه.

15: we have given شیمه in the transcription, but the ی is unusual.

16: the س and ل of تسلیم are minimized.

جناب جلالت و نبالت دستگاه فخامت و نجابت همراه استظهارا دوستان مشفقا مهربانا

روز قبل که عالیجاه محمد بیک همراه ملاقات صاحب مذکور رفته بود آن جناب مشفق معظم

فرموده بودند در باب احتمال اینکه در ملاحظه جزیره محمره نوشته شده باشد آن جناب هم

در مراسله جزیره محمره نوشته بودند مقصود دولت این جانب هم همان جزیره محمره است

در قلعه جدید ... همان مراسله دوستدار را در باب آن جناب نوشته است

ارسال داشت در ملاحظه نامه در اصل منظور همان ساختن قلعه در جزیره خارک

نوشته است نه محمره در واقع یکی است و ... جناب ... را

قبل از ورود ... دولت علیه در جزیره خارک قلعه ...

و ... آن جزیره مزبوره قلعه بنا کنند و حال آنکه اطلاع ندارد در مراسله

آن جناب محرر و نوشته است ... لفظ جزیره خارک را محمره نوشته است

محاله کرده مراسله دوستدار را با مراسله آن جناب ... ارسال داشت

در ملاحظه ... زیاده چه زحمت دهد

۱ جناب جلالت و نبالت و کفایت نصاباً محبان استظهارا دوستان اعتضادا مُشفقا مُعظّما
۲ از قراریکه عالیجاه مجدت ہمراه طامسن صاحب مذکور ساخت انجناب مُشفق مُعظّم
۳ فرموده اند که باحتمال اینکه در کاغذ دوستدار جزیرهٔ مُحمّره نوشته شده باشد
انجناب ہم
٤ در مراسله جزیرهٔ محمّره نوشته اند و مقصود اصلی انجناب ہم ہمان جزیرهٔ محمّره
بوده است
۵ که قلعه ساخته نشود   لہذا سواد ہمان مراسلهٔ دوستداررا که بانجناب نوشته است
٦ ارسال داشت که ملاحظه نمایند که اصل منظور ہمان نساختن قلعه در جزیرة الخزر
۷ بوده است نه محمّره که فے الواقع یکے است   و ہم دریںباب بخصوصه سر کار
اعلیحضرت پادشاہی
۸ قبول فرمودند که اولیای ایندولت علیه در جزیرة الخزر قلعه نسازند و دولت علیهٔ
روم
۹ در ساحل محاذی ان جزیرهٔ مزبوره قلعه بنا نکنند و حال انکه قطع دارد در مراسلهٔ
۱۰ انجناب محرر و نویسنده اشتباہاً لفظ جزیرة الخزررا مُحمّره نوشته است   باری
۱۱ عجالةً سواد مراسلهٔ دوستداررا با مراسلهٔ انجناب که خواہش رفته بود ارسال داشت
۱۲ که ملاحظه فرمایند   زیاده چه زحمت دہد

Vahed-e Nashr-e Asnad 1369 I, p. 419.

Notes

This example is particularly rich in diacritical marks, some of which are difficult to recognize. The familiar superscript mark appears in lines 5, 7, and 10, signalling a change of topic: we have used spaces to indicate these breaks. For الخزر in lines 6, 8, and 10, see Guide no. 26.

Line by line:

10: the tashdid and zamma of محرر appear to be reversed.

12: for a discussion of the squiggle following دہد see Guide no. 10.

جناب مستطاب اجل اکرم ارفع امجد اشرف عالی را با نهایت شوق زیارت میکنم

بعد اصل و تمام مراسلات جناب مستطاب عالی بالمره است و ادراکی مبادرت مستطیع کما حاصل

مخصوص در حضور مبارک اعلیحضرت همایون شاهنشاهی معروض داریم

اعلیحضرت همایون شاهنشاهی اراده ملوکانه بر رفع و دفع انها رفق صدور یافته بودند در خصوص

بعضی از اولیای دولت اعلیحضرت پادشاه ولیعهد تا بحال مسکوت ماندیم و لیکن همین حال از جناب

تلگراف وصول عنوان و بنا به خبر عمال انگاریه در آن تلگراف اظهار داشتند در خصوص

انگلستان در باب هر مسئله پیدا شده ایلچی دولت ایران مقیم لندن صلاح دانند و دولت ترتیب

بعد از آن خانه لندن حاضر خواهند بود به سفیر ایران نصیحت دهند لکن قاعده تا لرد سالزبوری باید

عمق آنرا نصیحت دهند و دفعه دیگر بار روزنامه های انگلیس ترجمه اعتنایی باشد کردند اگر چه هیچ معلوم

آن دولت باشد

محکم این فقرات یکجا منوط به حضوری است والبته میل داشت که انگلیس برای

مطالب از این [illegible] انگلیس این مطالعه منصوب [illegible]

اظهارات خواهشمندم اصل شرح [illegible] در لندن جمال الدین [illegible] مسائل همایون [illegible] لرد سالزبوری مستطاب [illegible] اعلیحضرت [illegible]

[illegible]

۱ جناب مستطاب اجل اکرم ارفع امجد اشرف عالے را با نهایت شوق و مسرت بتصدیع
مطالعه این نکارش مزاحم میکرداند
۲ امیدوارم مزاج جناب مستطاب عالے سالم است و از کرمی مسافرت خستکے کلے
حاصل نفرموده ائید خواهشمندم احترامات
۳ مخصوص مرا حضور مبارک اعلیحضرت همایون شاهنشاهے معروض دارید در
مسئله نکارشات جمال الدین در لندن
٤ اعلیحضرت همایون شاهنشاهے اراده ملوکانه بر رفع و دفع انها شرف صدور یافته
بود و بلا تعویق منظور همایونی را
٥ بحضور اولیای دولت اعلیحضرت پادشاه ولینعمت تاجدارم مکشوف ساختم و در
همین حال از جناب مستطاب لرد سالزبوری
٦ تلکراف وصول نمودم و بنا بدستور العمل اشعاریه در آن تلکراف اظهار می شود که
دولت اعلیحضرت پادشاه
۷ انکلستان در باب هر مسئله چاپ شده که ایلچیِ دولت ایران مقیم لندن صلاح داند که
در این باب رجوع
۸ بعدالت خانه بشود حاضر خواهند بود به سفیر ایران نصیحت دهند لکن قاعدتاً لرد
سالزبوری بهیچ دولت خارجه
۹ نمیتوانند نصیحت دهد و در باره نکارشات روزنامه های انکلیز شرح ادعایه پیش
کیرند اکرچه حق هم بطرف
۱۰ آن دولت باشد حکم این فقرات بکلے منوط به جوری است و البته میدانید در
انکلیز رای

Turn the page and read along the margin

۱۱ عموم بقدری مخالف این کونه ادعاهای پلیتیکے است
۱۲ که ندرتاً اتفاق میافتد که جوری
۱۳ حکم بر ضد روزنانه نکار میدهند
۱٤ زیاده زحمت است
۱٥ دوست حقیقے صمیمی جناب مستطابعالے
۱٦ فرنك لاسلس
۱۷ قلهك ششم جون ۱۸۹۲

Safa'i 1346, p. 272.

Notes

This example shows certain features of ta'liq style, such as the marked leftward slope, deeply curved final ـب-forms, and long diagonals for ک. (For examples of the ta'liq style, see Faza'eli 1350: 411–17). Final silent ه has a long hook. Final ن is not recurved. The shekasta logograph for شد is not used. The heads of ح-forms are usually minimized. The pen allowed no variation in the thickness of penstrokes.

In this example, and in Ex. 32 and 34, an effort has been made to keep the words separate and not run them together. Some of the most difficult letters to read in this hand are the ی in می شود in line 6 and in پیش in line 9. In each case the ی is a slanting stroke, not connected, with one or two dots below it.

A change of topic is signalled in line 3 by a space, and in line 10 by a space and a conventional mark.

Line by line:

1: امجد could possibly be read as اجمل. The order of مطالعه این appears to be reversed.

3: In شاہنشاہی the pen left the paper at the tooth of ن; see also the next line.

6: العمل presents a clear example of an initial upward ا.

9: although دهند would be expected, دهد was written: compare دهند in line 8. In پیش the pen left the paper at the tooth of ی.

10: جوری: jury.

13: the mark below the م of حکم is unexplained.

16: the ۳ written above the س (twice) of لاسلس was a convention in Iran and Afghanistan to distinguish س from any other letter. See Exx. 54:17, 57, 58, and Guide no. 78.

ظل اللهی   این روزها بعضی اخبار رسیده که [illegible] عرض رسیده

که خیلی مایهٔ تعجب و حیرت است که چرا مردم بی جهت و بی سبب آنچه که

در اقتدار و امنیت [illegible] کرده‌اند دنبال این نوع کارهای بی معنی

و خطرناک رفته شده [illegible] عرض رسیده که مردم بر ضد رعایای خارجه

در فرنگستان حرف می‌زنند و هم چنین عملهٔ اعلام اشتعال و [illegible]

[illegible] دارند و هم چنین در فقرهٔ بابی‌ها مزخرفات می‌گویند

و هرگاه باز دعوی و مردم این فقره را بپرانند که دولت [illegible] بابی‌ها

در حق رعیت که هم مهمان شرایع و آنچه که آن‌ها مطالبه

و باز بپرانند که اگر در امر دولت بپرانند که حافظ مملکت و استقلال

سلطنت و شریعت ضرری ملاحظه بپرانید اول کسی که در دفع آن بکوشد

دولت است که [illegible] هر کسی در کاری که دولت بکند اجرا و ارسو

مصلحت سرایر باز بپرانند که آن کار مصلحت مملکت و رعیت

و دولت است و ابدا چون و چرایی برای آن نباید

دولت حافظ مملکت و رعیت و حقوقش که هم حال خارجه و مهمان

شده‌اند اگر از اینها باشد و بر ضد احکام دولت حرکت بکنند

مطلقا که مهمان نفوس و حیات [illegible] و البته همه اشخاص

ثابت و راسخ [illegible] در این خصوص لازم و لابد [illegible] عهده

ملاحظه و لازم [illegible] در همه مقام آنچه لازم است بکنید

[illegible]

۱ ظل السلطان   این روزها بعضی اخبارات از اصفهان بعرض رسیده است
۲ که خیلی جای تعجب و حیرت است که چرا مردم بے جهة و سبب آسوده کے
۳ و راحتی و امنیت خود را کنار کذاشته دنبال این نوع کارهای بے معنی
٤ و خطرناک بروند مثلاً بعرض رسیده است که مردم بر ضد رعایای خارجه
۵ و فرنکیان حرف میزنند   و هم چنین علمای اعلام استعمال دخانیات
٦ را حرام دانسته اند   و هم چنین در فقره بانك نو مزخرفات میکویند
۷ اولاً باید شما و علما و مردم این فقره را بدانند که دولت و شخص پادشاه
۸ در حق رعیت از همه مهربان تر است و آسوده کے ان ها را طالب
۹ و باید بدانند که اکر در امری دولت بداند که برای مملکت و استقلال
۱۰ سلطنت و شریعت ضرری وارد بیاید اول کسی که در دفع ان بکوشد
۱۱ دولت است   پس هر حکمی و کاری که دولت میکند و اجرای اورا
۱۲ مصلحت میداند باید بدانند که ان کار مصلحت مملکت و رعیت
۱۳ و دولت است و ابداً چون و چرائے بر زبان نیاورند
۱٤ دولت برای مملکت و رعیت خودش از همه دل سوزتر و مهربان
۱۵ تر است و اکر غیر این باشد و بر ضد احکام دولت سخن بکویند
۱٦ واضح است که منتهای فضولے و جسارت است و البته همچه اشخاص
۱۷ تنبیه و تادیب و سیاست سختی را لازم دارند و بر عهده دولت
۱۸ واجب و لازم می شود که در همچه مقام انچه لازمه کیفر

Turn page upside down and read from the top down:

۱۹ و مجازات سخت است
۲۰ بمردم نادان بدهد
۲۱ و بفهماند که خلاف احکام
۲۲ دولت را کسی نمی تواند
۲۳ بکند   در فقره عمل
۲٤ تنباکو و دخانیات
۲۵ قرار نامهٔ با
۲٦ کمپانے آن کار بسته شده است
۲۷ که سواد ان در پیش

٢٨ شما حاضر است چرا
٢٩ نمی دہید مردم
٣٠ ملاحظه نمایند
٣١ البته بعد ز دیدن
٣٢ ان قرار دادہا
٣٣ خواہند فہمید که چقدر
٣٤ دقت در آن
٣٥ کار شده است که به
٣٦ احدی ضرری وارد
٣٧ نیاید

Safa'i 1346, p. 11.

Notes

A draft of a telegram in the hand of Naser al-Din Shah. Many dots are lacking. است is often written ideographically (see, e.g., line 1). Conventional superscript marks appear frequently to signal changes of topic; we have indicated this by a space except at the beginning of lines 7 and 9. Upright ر is seen in وارد in lines 10 and 36, and in قرار in lines 25 and 32.

Line by line:

7: باید is written in a form indistinguishable from باد.

16: the form ہمچه is notable because it appears to be a written form of a colloquial pronunciation: see also line 18.

31: the ا of از is lacking.

جناب جلالتمآب اجل اکرم اشرف ... افخم ... مکرم

التماس ... که اعلیحضرت اقدس شهریاری در باب منصب ... شرف

مشیرالدوله ... وزیر امور خارجه بخدمت جناب جلالتمآب اجل اکرم افخم ... دارند

... جناب جلالتمآب معظم له اظهار ...

در ... اعلیحضرت ... اعلیحضرت اقدس شهریاری ... ۱۳۰۸

... جناب جلالتمآب اجل اشرف ... ربیع الثانی ۹۴

١ جناب مستطاب جلالتماب اجل اکرم اشرف را با کمال احترام زحمت افزا می کردد
٢ اطميناناتيکه اعليحضرت اقدس شهرياری در باب منصوب نکردن جناب اشرف
٣ مشير الدوله بمنصب وزير امور خارجکے داده بودند خدمت جناب جلالتماب اجل اکرم
افخم لار سالزبری
٤ تلکراف کردم جناب جلالتماب معظم اليه اظهار رضايت نموده و علاوه بر آن
٥ ذکر نموده اند که دولت اعليحضرت پادشاه انکلستان کاملاً مُطمئن باين وعده
اعليحضرت اقدس شهرياری ميباشند
٦ محض استحضار جناب جلالتماب اجل اشرف زحمت افزا کرديد فے ٩ ربيع الثانے
١٣٠٨

Safa'i 1346, p. 150.

Notes

Line by line:

2: the mark over اطمينانات generally indicates the beginning of a new topic, and here seems to signal the beginning of the body of the text.

3: داده is written as one penstroke, with a hook under the ه. It is difficult to say why داده بودند is stacked in the middle of the line unless the words were forgotten at the time of writing and added later. لارد either lacks its د, or is spelled لرد as in Ex. 31:5, 8.

5: the dots of the ش of ميباشد are stacked so high that it is easy to misread them as belonging to what is above. پادشاه is written with two penstrokes: پادشا and ه, with the ه located below the گ of انگلستان. The diagonal of the ک of کاملاً interferes with انگلستان.

6: The diagonal of the ک of گرديد touches the و of وعده in the line above.

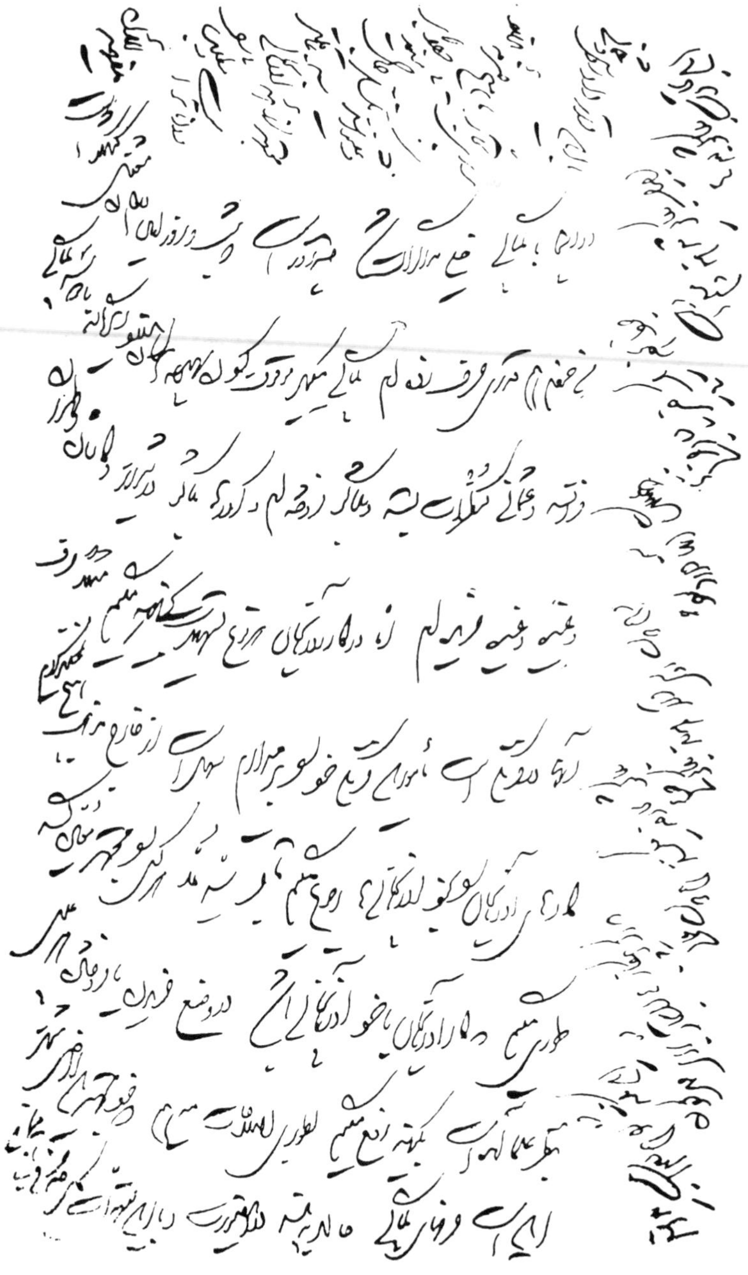

١ در اینجا با کمپانی خیلی مذاکرات شد چند روز است که شب و روز امین السلطان
مشغول کفتکو است

٢ من خودم هم قدری حرف زده ام کمپانی میکوید موقوف کردن بهیچوجه امکان ندارد
زیراکه با دو سه ٣ کمپانی

٣ فرانسه و عثمانی کنطرات بسته و تنباکو فروخته ام وکرورها تنباکو در شیراز و
کاشان و طهران

٤ و غیره و غیره خریده ام امّا در کار آذربایجان هر نوع تسهیلات بخواهید میکنم مثلاً
حرف

٥ آنها در فرنگی است مأمورین فرنگی خودرا بر میدارم سهل است از خارج مذهب هیچ
نمیکذارم

٦ کارهای آذربایجان را بخود اذربایجانی ها رجوع میکنم تاجر سیّد ملاّ هر کس را
مجتهد مُعین کند

٧ طوری میکنم که کار آذربایجان با خود آذربایجانی باشد در وضع خریدن یا فروختن
هر عیبی

٨ بنظر علما آمده است بکویند رفع میکنم بطوری اصلاحات میدهم که خود مجتهدین
راضی شوند

٩ این است حرفهای کمپانی حالا ببینید در اینصورت و با این تعهّدات دیکر چه حرفی
باقی میماند

Turn the page and read along the right margin beginning at the left-hand line

١٠ این نکته را هم لازم است بدانید

١١ که اکر اینکارها را تجّار برای حمل کردن

١٢ تنباکو بخارجه میکنند هم دولت عثمانی

١٣ و هم دولت روس قرار نهاده اند (؟) تنباکوئی که

١٤ بمملکت آنها وارد شود

١٥ ضبط نموده یك چیز بسیار جزئی

١٦ بصاحب تنباکو بدهند و مُسلّم است

١٧ این تجارت تنباکو بعدها

Turn the page and read across the top margin

١٨ با این قرارداد روس و عثمانی

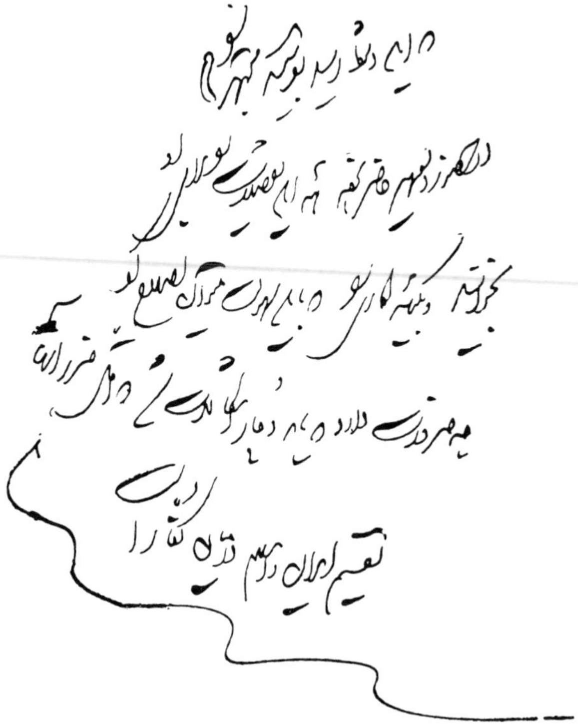

۱۹ برای تجّار ما هیچ صرفهٔ ندارد
۲۰ و نمیتوانند بکنند حاجی سید جواد اقای
۲۱ مجتهد از همهٔ آذربایجانے عاقلتر
۲۲ و داناتر است و مطلب ما را
۲۳ میفهمد الآن

Continued

۲٤ که این دستخط رسید بفرستید مجتهدرا هم
۲۵ در حضور ولیعهد حاضر نموده همهٔ این تفصیلات را برای او
۲٦ بخوانید و بکوئید کاری را که باین سهولت میتوان اصلاح کرد
۲۷ چه ضرورت دارد که باید دُچار اشکالات شد که اقلّ ضرر آنها
۲۸ تقسیم ایران و اسلام در میان کفّار است

Safa’i 1346, pp. 17–18.

Notes

A draft of a telegram in the hand of Amin al-Soltan, dating from the beginning of the tobacco crisis. The style involves a great deal of exaggeration and minimization, combined with other idiosyncratic features. For example, ه generally has a very long hook below it: see, e.g., هم in line 2. Final ت is often superscribed and exaggerated. The diagonal of ک is long and curves back. Zamma is often exaggerated and resembles the symbol for three dots (see گفتگو in line 1). Initial ح-forms are greatly minimized. The و of خود is usually not visible. Single dots, double dots, and single dots over adjacent letters are often rendered as a straight line, sometimes greatly exaggerated.

Line by line:

1: the logograph for شد runs into the ت of مذاکرات. The ا of السلطان is written below the word.

3: کنطرات: contract.

١ جناب اشرف اتابك اعظم تلكرافها را ديدم انشا اله با فضل خداوند
٢ و حسن تدبير شما اميدم اين است تمام اين خرابيها اصلاح شود
٣ ولے در فقرهٔ پول اينكه نوشته ايد وزير ماليه ديروز در مجلس مذاكرات
٤ كرده است ندانستم نتيجه اقدامات و مذاكرات او چه شده
٥ و مجلس در اينخصوص چه قرار نهاده است از همه امورات امروز مهم تر
٦ اين كار است خوب بود ما حصل كفتكوى مجلس را در اينخصوص
٧ امروز بمن اطلاع مى داديد كه معلوم شود وعده ها چه شده است

Turn the page and read along the margin

٨ و انشا اله
٩ بعد از (؟) رسيدن سردار مكرم
١٠ درين شهر (؟) سالار الدوله هم
١١ تكليف خودش را دانسته
١٢ و بلكه (؟) انشا اله بمسالمت
١٣ اين كار اصلاح شود

Safa'i 1346, p. 403.

Notes

A letter in the hand of Mohammad 'Ali Shah.

Line by line:

2: the **ميد** of **اميد** is merely a curved line: cf. **رسيدن** in line 9.

7: the reading **وعده ها** is uncertain.

9: the reading **بعد از** is uncertain.

10: the reading **درين شهر** is uncertain.

12: the reading **و بلكه** is uncertain; **ديگر** has also been suggested.

IV

The following fifteen examples from India and Iran, dating from around 1900, are drawn from Levy 1951 and *Specimens* 1902.

۱۳۱۵

۱۲ شهر ربیع الثانی

خدمت جناب مستطاب آقای ضیاء الاطباء دام اقباله العالی

تشرف عرض عالی میرساند رقیمه مطالعه مبارک زیارت گردید از استقامت مزاج

مبارک بکمال خوشوقتی دست داد و از اینکه تشریف آورده و برای پذیرائی

حاضر نبوده ام خیلی متاسف شدم و از محضر مبارک معذرت میخواهم

برای تشریف فرمائی جناب جلالتمآب اجل اکرم عالی آقای

ضیاء الملک دام اقباله العالی به بنده منزل وقت خواسته بودید

روز شنبه چهاردهم دو ساعت بغروب مانده در منزل

خودم برای پذیرائی جناب معظم الیه با کمال میل

و افتخار حاضرم زیاده عرضی ندارد ایام بکام مستدام باد

١ ١٢ شهر ربيع الاول ١٣١٥
٢ خدمت جناب مستطاب آقای ضیاء الاطباء دام اقباله العالی
٣ بشرفعرض عالیمیرساند رقیمه مطاعه مبارک زیارت کردید از استقامت مزاج
٤ مبارک کمال خوشوقتی دست داد از اینکه تشریف آورده و برای پذیرائی
٥ حاضر نبوده ام خیلی متاسّف شدم و از محضر مبارک معذرت میخواهم
٦ برای تشریف فرمائی جناب جلالتماب اجل اکرم عالی آقای
٧ ضیاء الملك دام اقباله العالی به بنده منزل وقت خواسته بودید
٨ روز شنبه چهاردهم دو ساعت بغروب مانده در منزل
٩ خودم برای پذیرائی جناب معظم الیه با کمال میل
١٠ و افتخار حاضرم زیاده عرضی ندارد ایام شوکت مستدام باد

Levy 1951, p. 116.

Notes

This letter, written to the Chief Physician of the Persian court, provides a convenient transition from the bureaucratic writing of the earlier examples to personal writing for everyday purposes. There is no signature, which in the case of this type of document may have been written on the envelope only. Though small, the writing is neat and elegant, with stacking at the end of each line that fills in the space between lines and creates a consistent left margin. The formulaic nature of much of the language encourages simplifications such as the omission of dots and the linking of words.

Line by line:

1: in the ligature of ول in الاول, the ل barely rises vertically.

3: in the first part of the line the boilerplate is run together.

5: the small diacritic ک over the elongated dish of the ک of مبارک prevents it from being misread as a dotless ت.

عالیجاه بلند جایگاه دوست مکرم مهربان من

مراسله مهر آیات مودت سمات آن مکرم

دوست مهربان سمت وصول یافته و از شرح مسطورات و فحاوی اظهارات مودت طراز آن مندرجه

خاطر دوستی اثر مستحضر و چون در ضمن آن بشارت صحت و عافیت مزاج شریف مفهوم و معلوم بود

زایدالوصف مبتهج و مستبشر شد و در ذیل مراحم و عواطف بیکران اعلیحضرت قدر قدرت قوی شوکت

شاهنشاه جمجاه ارواحنا فداه باعطای لقب جلیل تبریک و تهنیت نموده بودید همواره از مراتب مودت

و درجات یکجهتی و اتحاد آن دوست مکرم اطمینان و خبری حاصل است و در هیچ موقعی این دوست صادق خود را

فراموش نکرده‌اید و تلگرافا نیز در اظهار محبت نموده تبریک فرموده بودید در مدارج خشنودی خود را از طرز مودت

آن دوست مکرم اظهار داشته بود و اکنون نیز حقیقت انبساط و مراتب امتنان خاطر خود را

از مهربانیهای آن دوست مکرم در تلو این نگارش معلوم رای شریف میدارد زیاده زحمت است

۱۹ شعبان المعظم ۱۳۰۶

١ عالیجاه بلند جایگاه دوست مکرم مهربان من مراسله دوستی ایات مودت سمات ان مکرم
٢ دوست مهربان سمت وصول یافته و از شرح مسطورات و فحاوی اظهارات که در طی ان مندرج بود
٣ خاطر دوستی اثر مستحضر و چون در ضمن ان بشارت صحت و عافیت مزاج شریف مفهوم و معلوم بود
٤ زاید الوصف مبتهج و مستبشر شد در بذل مراحم و عواطف بندکان علیحضرت قدر قدرت قضا شوکت
٥ شاهنشاه جمجاه ارواحنا فداه با عطای لقب جلیل تبریك و تهنیت نموده بودید همواره از مراتب مودت
٦ و درجات یکجهتی و اتحاد ان دوست مکرم امتنان و خرمی حاصل است که در هیچ موقع این دوست صادق خودرا
٧ فراموش نکرده اید و تلگرافا نیز که اظهار محبت نموده تبریك فرموده بودند مدارج خشنودی خودرا از طرز مودت
٨ ان دوست مکرم اظهار داشته بود و اکنون نیز حقیقت انبساط و مراتب امتنان خاطر خودرا
٩ از مهربانے ان دوست مکرم در تلو این نکارش معلوم رای شریف میدارد زیاده زحمت است ١٩ شعبان المُعظم ١٣٠٦

Specimens 1902, p. 155.

Notes

Dots are often clustered, as in عالیجاه and جایگاه in line 1, and یافته in line 2.

Line by line:

2: اظهارات shows how ط and ظ can be written in shekasta with ه incorporated within them. See also lines 7, 8.

وقایع اتفاقیه دارالعلم شیراز از تاریخ روز یکشنبه دهم شهر رجب المرجب سنه ۱۳۱۸ مطابق

چهارم ماه نومبر سنه ۱۹۰۰ کارهای حکومتی از قرار سابق است جناب مشیرالملک

شخصاً مشغول جمع کردن بقایای مالیات هستند هر یک از ملاک و عمال و ضباط را

میفرستند بیاورند بدفترخانه حاضر کرده حساب او را میکشند هرچه باقی مالیات او باشد

بفرض هم که خیلی جزئی باشد او را نگاه میدارند تا ادا در [illegible] مرخص میکنند

امسال جناب معزی الیه خوب مالیاتی جمع کرده هر ساله این موقع هنوز چهار پنجماه بابت مالیات

مبالغ کلی باقی مالیات هرجا بود لکن امسال هیچ محلی تاکنون چندان باقی نمانده

١ روزنامچه

٢ وقایع اتفاقیه دار العلم شیراز از تاریخ روز یکشنبه دہم شہر رجب المرجب سنه ۱۳۱۸ مطابق

٣ چہارم ماه نومبر سنه ۱۹۰۰ کارہای حکومتی از قرار سابق است جناب مُستشار الماک

٤ بسختی مشغول جمع کردن بقایای مالیات ہستند ہر يك از ملاک و عمال و ضبّاط را

٥ میفرستند میاورند بدفتر خانه حاضر کرده حساب اورا می کنند ہرچه باقے مالیاتے او باشد

٦ بر فرض ہم که خیلے جزئے باشد اورا نکاه می دارند از او دریافت کرده مرخص می کنند

٧ امساله جنابمعزی الیه خوب مالیاتے جمع کردند ہر ساله این موقع که ہنوز چہار پنجماه بسال مانده است

٨ مبالغ کلے باقے مالیات ہر جا بود لیکن امسال ہیچ محلے تا کنون چندآن باقے ندارد

Specimens 1902, p. 29.

Notes

Dots are often clustered: see, e.g., اتفاقیه in line 1 and بسختی in line 4. Original reduced 20%.

Line by line:

1: روزنامچه is written with four penstrokes: ر, و (extended and curled up), زنا (see Guide no. 43), and مچه (lacking dots).

3: the conventional mark above کار ہا signals the beginning of the body of the letter.

5: note the form of کرده in lines 5 and 6.

جناب فخامت و مناعت انتسابا دوستان اشرف اشفقا معظما مهربانا

مراسله مودت مواصله که از فرط محبت و اتحاد نگاشته بودید واصل گردید فی الواقع

از مراتب محبت و حق‌شناسی جناب جلالت‌مآب اجل آقای وزیر دام اقباله العالی نهایت

تشکر و امتنان قلبی حاصل نمود که بعد از تشریف فرمائی دماوند تجدید زیارت ارادتمند

ارادتمند فائز نشده‌اند اگرچه مراتب ارادت و اخلاص بنده به هیچ‌وجه نسبت

بشخص محترم معظم‌له بدون ملاحظه چیزی و مخصوصاً از صمیم قلب است ولی

باز از عطای مرقومه ممتاز نمودن معظم‌له بر مراتب ارادت سابقه

صمیمی به نهایت افزوده شد امیدوار است که همواره اوقات سلسله مودت

و اتحاد قلبی فیمابین پاینده و مستدام بوده باشد در این موقع تکرار احترامات فائقه مبادرت

١ جناب فخامت و مناعت انتسابا دوستان استظهارا مشفقا معظما مهربانا
٢ مراسلهٔ مودّت مواصلهٔ که از فرط محبت واتحاد نکاشته شده بود واصل کردید فے الواقع
٣ از مراتب محبت و حق شناسی جناب جلالتماب اجل اقای وزیر دام اقباله العالے نهایت
٤ تشکر و امتنان قلبی حاصل نمود که بعد از تشریف فرمائے و مسافرت بعید باز از یاد
٥ ارادتمند فارغ نبوده اند اکرچه مراتب ارادت و اخلاص بنده هم نسبت
٦ بشخص محترم معظم الیه بدون ملاحظهٔ چیزی و مخصوصاً از صمیم قلب است ولے
٧ باز از اعطاء یکقبضه تفنك ممتاز مرحمتی معظم الیه بر مراتب ارادت سابقه
٨ صمیمی بے نهایت افزوده شد امیدوار است که هموارهٔ اوقات سلسلهٔ مودت
٩ واتحاد قلبی فیمابین پاینده و مستدام بوده باشد در این موقع تجدید احترامات فائقه را مینماید

Specimens 1902, p. 83.

Notes

Minimization is a feature throughout, especially in the formulaic phrases. Note especially the first line, فارغ in line 5, سلسله in line 8, and the final words of line 9. In محبت in line 3 and نسبت at the end of line 5, the final ت approximates the ta'liq form rather than the nasta'liq.

The presence of dots helps overcome the difficulties of reading: see, e.g., جناب in lines 1 and 3, or تشریف in line 4.

Line by line:

3: the tail below the م of جلالتماب is unexplained.

5: there is no final د in ارادتمند.

9: فائقه را is difficult to read because the ر touches the preceding ه. For the flourish below the end of the line, see Guide no. 10.

۱۸ رمضان
۱۳۱۲

جناب مستطاب اجل اکرم وزیر مختار دولت بهیه انگلیس دام اجلاله

بتقاضای کمال مودت باین مختصر زحمت میدهم که رقیمه

و از نوشته جناب مستطاب شنیده ام

هم سابق بخدمت دوستانه جواب نوشته بودم

بنظر رسیده است و البته هر ترتیبی که را

خاطر عالی مستحضر است فرموده اند محض اطلاع زحمت دادم

١ ١٨ شهر رمضان ١٣١٧

٢ جناب مستطاب اجل اكرم وزير مختار دولت قوى شوكت بهيه انكليس
دام اجلاله

٣ باقتضاى كمال مودّت باين مختصر زحمت ميدهم

٤ و از سلامت جناب مستطابعالے استفسار مينمايم سه فقره پاكت

٥ هم سابق بدفعات فرستاده ام كه جواب هيچكدام

٦ بمن نرسيده است و البته هر سه ٣ پاكت را

٧ جنابعالے ملاحظه فرموده ايد محض اطلاع زحمت دادم ...

Specimens 1902, p. 117.

Notes

Many letters are minimized and many teeth or letters are simply not present. Lacking entirely are, e.g., the ت of مستطاب in lines 2 and 4 and the ت of فرستاده ام in line 5, although the dots are present in each case. Almost invisible are the ت of اقتضا and of مختصر, and the initial م of ميدهم in line 3. Very small are, typically, the با of باين in line 3 and the پا of پاكت in lines 4 and 6. The squiggle to the right of line 6 is illegible. A similar squiggle appears in Ex. 48:12. See Guide no. 10.

Line by line:

5: the ام of فرستاده ام is a single penstroke: cf. اند of فرموده اند in line 7.

7: the words following دادم are likely to be a formula such as زياده فدايت but the reading is uncertain.

۲۴ شهر شوال المکرم

رقیمهٔ محترمهٔ جنابعالی با پست دیروز رسید زیارت شد

شرف وصول یافت از شرحی که در باب سعی بزرگان سیاست

در ایام ملک مرحوم نوشته بودید مختصر شرحی چون طرفین با اختلاف اظهار داشته‌اند

که برطبق اظهارات خود بمهمات سببی منعقد نهند اثرات را از حق قانون

راجع به مجلس محترم و ملکات شرعیه نمی‌پرسیم از حضور آن مجلس محترم طرفین را

به صلاح ملک و دیگر کیفیات سعادت سعیدی که قبول کرده در شمار اسم

شتر بساز در صیغهٔ مصالحه از طرفین اسم جاری نموده راضی

قضیهٔ مصالحه چند روز گذشت ابرا هم نمی اجرا نشر اظهار

که فرمایش شما تعهدات ابراز است که مرقوم داشته اید

١ ٢٤ شهر شوال المكرم

٢ فدايت شوم   رقيمه محترمه جنابعالے با كمال مسرّت و خوشوقتى

٣ شرف وصُول يافت   از شرحى كه در باب عمل بيوكخان سر تيپ

٤ و ابراهيم بك مرقوم داشته بوديد مُستحضر شد چون طرفين باختلاف اظهار ميداشتند

٥ كه بر طبق اظهارات خود متمسك بسندى نبودند   لهذا مراتب را بر حسب قانون

٦ راجع به محضر محترم محاكمات شرعيه نموده پس از حضور ان مجلس محترم
طرفين را

٧ اصلاح داده و بيوكخان مُعادل يكصد و سى تومان قبول كرده كه بمشار اليه

٨ مسترد سازد و صيغه مصالحه از طرفين باهم جارى شده بعد از اين

٩ قضيه و مصالحه چند روز كه كذشت ابراهيم بيك آمد اظهار داشت

١٠ كه من راضى نيستم تفصيل از اينقرار است ديكر دوستدار مطلع نيست

Specimens 1902, p. 143.

Notes

For the arrangement of lines on this page, see Guide no. 6. The zammas above مستحضر in line 4, معادل in line 7, and گذشت in line 9 are exaggerated.

Line by line:

3: the mark above در باب signals a change of topic.

4: the mark above چون is possibly a zamma.

5: the influence of the ta‘liq style can be seen in the ک of متمسك. See also the ک of بيك in line 9.

7: for the analysis of تومان, see Guide no. 43.

10: note the flourish below the end of the line; see Guide no. 10.

۲

مراسله شریفه را در باب تعیین نیابت شما

در خدمت جناب مستطاب اجل اکرم آقای صنیع الدوله دام اقباله العالی حفظه الله

نمود چون جناب معظم نظرشان مبنی بر بعضی ملاحظاتی است که تا او را

انجام مرحمت مساعدت نخواهند فرمود و در باب کشیش هم هیچ وجه خبری از

اتمام کارشان نرسیده با اینکه از دهم ماه به طرف ارومیه

سرحد و شطر خبر حرکتشان بوده هنوز بی اطلاع مانده ایم که از

چه وقت تشریف خواهند آورد بنابراین از تعیین درخواستشان

عذر میخواهم زیرا نمی توانم وقت را تحقیق و قول بدهم ترکمان

١ هو
٢ فدایت شوم مراسلهٔ شریفه را در باب تعیین
٣ ورود جناب مستطاب اجل اکرم آقای صنیع الدوله مد ظله العالے ملاحظه
٤ نمود چون جناب معظم سفرشان مبنی بر یك کاری است که تا اورا
٥ انجام ندہند معاودت نخواہند فرمود و تا کنون ہم بہیچوجه خبری از
٦ اتمام کارشان نرسیده با اینکه از دہم دسامبر باینطرف ہمه روزہا
٧ مترصد و منتظر خبر حرکتشان بوده معہذا بے اطلاع مانده و نمیداند
٨ چه وقت تشریف خواہند آورد بنا بر این از تعیین ورود ایشان
٩ عُذر میخواہد و نمی تواند وقتی را مشخص نماید و قول بدہد ...
١٠ مخبر السلطنه

Specimens 1902, p. 101.

Notes

Independent final ن lacks the dot.

Line by line:

3: the pen left the page in ظله.

6: for the زہا of روزها see Guide no. 43.

7: the conventional mark over معہذا signals a change of topic.

9: the words following بدہد may be a formula such as زیاده زحمت but the reading is unclear.

10: the signature is in a different hand from the rest of the text.

عرض می‌شود

نظر به اینکه معتمدین دولت متبوعه طرفین

همین جناب هم که زحمت کشیده در شب ۱۸ شهر حال در بدن محمد حسن فرج الحسن سعد سنه

جمعه الحمد لله عصره در عمارت بیرون تشریف ارزانی داشته

و به صرف شربت و چای این جانب را مسرور فرمایند

[illegible] شهر [illegible]

زیاده از این مطلبی نیست والسلام خیر ختام

[illegible]

١ عرضمی شود نظر به اتحاد معنوی و مودت باطنی
٢ متمنی چنانم که زحمت کشیده در شب ١٨ شهر حال در مجلس جشن قرة العین سعادت مند
٣ عبد المحمد طول لله عمره در عمارت بیرون تشریف شریف ارزانے داشته
٤ و بصرف شربت و چای این جانب را مسرور نمائید
٥ زیاده از این مطلبی نیست والسلام خیر اختتام فے ١٦ شهر ذی حجه
٦ ملك التجار

Specimens 1902, p. 21.

Notes

A straight left margin has been obtained by a considerable stacking of words in every line.

Line by line:

3: either the ا of الله is dropped or the second ل is not visible. The beginning parts of تشریف and شریف are minimized almost beyond recognition.

5: the last five words are stacked: reading from bottom to top they are: ١٦ فے شهر ذی حجه, with the حجه above the ذی.

6: the mark over ملك signals a personal name.

دوشنبه سه دی ماه
۱۳۱۷

دوست عزیزم [illegible]

دو سه ساعتی از وقت شریف [illegible] امروز صبح میخواستم

[illegible] قبول دعوت زحمت [illegible]

[illegible]

[illegible] زحمت [illegible] عذر میخواهم

امیدوارم [illegible] شرفیاب شوم

معذرت میخواهم [illegible]

١ دوشنبه ٨ شهر ذی حجه ١٣١٧
٢ فدایت شوم   کمال میل را داشتم که فردا را بقلهک آمده
٣ و دو سه ٣ ساعتی از اوقات شریف مسرور باشم امروز صبح میخواستم
٤ بجواب قبول دعوت زحمت بدهم امّا آثار کسالتی بروز کرد
٥ بعد نوبه و تب آمد تا بحال هنوز آسایش حاصل نشده است
٦ که بخط خودم هم نتوانستم زحمت بدهم و با کمال افسوس عذر میخواهم
٧ امیدوارم همین که حالتی پیدا کردم خودم شرفیاب شده
٨ معذرت بخواهم زیاده زحمتی نداده   حسن ...

Specimens 1902, p. 57

Notes

Line by line:

2: the dots beneath کمال are not explained.

8: the ه of نداده ends in a flourish (see Guide no. 10). The word below حسن is illegible.

سواد

از طرف کپیتان اشهندر بمحمد حسن بیک نائب سفارت

۴ اگست ۱۹۰۰
۷ ربیع الثانی ۱۳۱۸

جناب محمد حسن بیک قزلباش نائب سفارت رنجیده شدید تاکمال
دو سه مرتبه است بشما پیغام داده‌ام که باید بیائید در کنسلگری
سرحد مملکت خراسان دیدن شکیه باینجا آمده با کارگذار سفارت
بطوریکه مرخصی گرفته اید مقصد بروید و تاکمال
جواب صحیح بمن نداده اید لهذا اکیداً اطلاع مینویسم
که هرگاه تا ده روز دیگر از تاریخ این تلگراف نیامده
و در سفارت جهه را توضیح نکنید درباره شما اجراآت
دیگر خواهد شد زیاده مطلبی نیست ۷ ربیع الثانی ۱۳۱۸

١ سواد

٢ از طرف کپتان اشنیدر   بمحمد حسن بیك غلام سفارت

٣ ٤ اکست ۱۹۰۰   ۷ ربیع الثانے ۱۳۱۸

٤ عالیجاه محمد حسن بیك قزلباش غلام سفارت را قلمی میشود تا بحال

٥ دو سه ۳ مرتبه است بشما پیغام داده ام که باید بیائید در قلهك

٦ سر خدمت خودتان و یا اینکه باینجا آمده باستحضار سفارت

٧ بطوریکه مرخصی کرفته اید بمقصد بروید و تا بحال

٨ جواب صحیح بمن نداده اید   لهذا اکیداً بشما مینویسم

٩ که هر کاه تا دو روز دیکر از تاریخ ذیل بقلهك نیامده

١٠ و در سفارت جهة را توضیح نکنید در باره شما اقدامات

١١ دیکر خواهد شد زیاده نمینکارد فے ۷ شهر ربیع الثانے ۱۳۱۸

١٢ مطابق ٤ اکست سنه ۱۹۰۰

Specimens 1902, p. 99.

Notes

There is a diacritic mark above the ك of بيك in lines 2 and 4, and that of قلهك in lines 5 and 9.

Line by line:

5: the long ه of داده and the ligature of ام are noteworthy.

8: لهذا has a line above it indicating a new topic. The form of بشما should be noted.

10: جهت is written with *ta marbuta*: for a discussion of Arabic words in ta marbuta in Persian, see John R. Perry, *Form and Meaning in Persian Vocabulary: The Arabic Feminine Ending,* Costa Mesa, CA: 1991.

11: the words after ۱۳۱۸ are written in a different hand. For the mark between ۱۳۱۸ and اکست see Ex. 31:16, Exx. 57, 58, and Guide no. 78.

واز قرار

مرحمت جناب صدارتمآب اجل ارفع و فخامت نصاب محترم ... از درجات حاجی سپهسالار

مرحمت انجام می‌شود مرقومه ۱۸ جمادی الاول عریضه مخصوص میرزا ... خواهد

مرحمت الطاف حاجی سپهسالار تقدیم مخصوص ... جواب از ... پیشکش

همراهی از مرحمت جلالت مخصوص ... رضوی حاجی ...

یک تخم ... از ... به دستور ... جواب ... سپهسالار

در حقیقت ... لهذا ... داده ... جواب ...

صفر ۱۳۱۶

در ... معتضد ... مرحمت ... تحریر ...

١ خدمت جناب جلالتماب شوکت و فخامت نصاب دوست محترم مہربان شارژ دافر
صاحب بہادُر دام اقبالہُ

٢ زحمت افزا می شود   که مورخه ١٨ جُون عریضه مختصری مبنی از حالات خود

٣ خدمت انصاحب بہادُر تقدیم نموده و در باب جواب از دولت ہندوستان خواہش

٤ ہمراہی از خدمت جنابعالے نموده بود که یا جوابے زودتر حاصل فرمائید

٥ و یا غم خواری از دوستدار بکنید تا اکنون جوابے که سبب اطمینان باشد

٦ مرحمت نشده لہذا دو مراتبه زحمت داده خواہش جواب مینماید

٧ که بہر قرار مقتضی میدانند جوابے مرحمت بفرمایند تحریر ٢٧ ربیع الاخر ١٣١٨

In the right margin ٨ سردار عبد الخالق خان

Specimens 1902, p. 53.

Notes

The marks at the head of the page are unexplained but are in the position where ہو could be expected. The thick strokes in the writing contrast strongly with the thin ones and in some cases they smooth out teeth, such as that for the ن of جناب in lines 2 and 5, the ت of ہندوستان in line 4. The bowl of final ن is almost closed. The form of ا in مہربان in line 2, in باب in line 4, and in ویا in line 6 should be noted (see Guide no. 43).

Line by line

1: the zamma over بہادر is exaggerated: see also line 3.

3: in در باب the first penstroke is ودر.

5: the dots of the ش of باشد are a vertical stroke. See also نشده in line 7.

6: the د of نشده is extended and suggests a ر. The unorthodox plural مراتبه following a numeral probably reflects vernacular usage.

7: ربیع is minimized. The خر of الاخر is written above, with the ر extended horizontally.

جناب نورچشمی حیدر [illegible] قلی [illegible]

در شب سه شنبه جمعه نهم شهر [illegible]

در شب [illegible] جناب آقا محمد مهدی [illegible] به جناب شیخ صفر [illegible]

شیخ صفر عرض احوال [illegible]

اینکه [illegible]

در شب [illegible] جناب آقا محمد مهدی [illegible]

خدمت [illegible] شما که [illegible] شیخ صفر [illegible] آقا محمد مهدی [illegible]

١ عاليجاه نور چشمی حیدر قلے خان را قلمی میشود نوشته مورخه جمعۀ نهم
بتاریخ سه شنبه بیستم رسید و از مطالب مندرجه استحضار حاصل کردید
٢ نوشته بودید چند یوم است عالیجاه آقا محمد مهدی وارد شده و عالیجاه شیخ صقر را
خواسته است بیاید بندر که در آنجا بگفتکوی عارضین رسیدکے نماید اگر
٣ شیخ صقر ناخوشی احوال نبود و از آمدن بندر متعذر نمی شد و بنا این بود که با
حضور شما باین امر رسیدکے شود البته حکمی هم بافتخار شما صادر می شد
٤ اینکه شما را بالمرّه بیدخل کردم مقصود این بود که ساعت آخر حرفے برای شما
نباشد حالا که از اینقرار راه حرفے برای خود درست کرده اید با اینکه صریحاً از
پیش بشما
٥ نوشته بودم که بورود آنجا بفاصله دو ٢ سه ٣ روز عالیجاه آقا محمد مهدی باید برود
بجزیره قشم ندانستم چه قسم شده که آنجا توقف کرده خلاصه اکر باجتهاد شما
بوده
٦ خوب کاری نشده شما که میدانستید شیخ صقر عذر ناخوشی دارد و بندر نمی آید در
اینصورت چرا بیوجه آقا محمد مهدی معطل شده باشد زیاده زحمت است

Specimens 1902, p. 147.

Notes

The marks at the head of the page are unexplained but some have suggested that they represent هو الله. Original reduced 5%.

Line by line:

3: the conventional mark above بنا signals a change of topic.

5: the numerals ٢ and ٣ are written above the words for them, as is now common. In آنجا the madda and the dot for the ن are written high above the word.

۱۳۱۷

مورخه ۲۵ شهر شوال المکرم

مطابق

۲۶ شهر فبروری ۱۹۰۰

بعرض حضور مبارک میرسانم اولاً همواره از درگاه حضرت احدیت در حراست [illegible] مسئلت مینماید

که وجود مسعود مبارک حضرت مستطاب اجل اکرم افخم عالی روحنا فداه را از کافه حوادث محفوظ فرماید

ثانیاً معروض میدارد مدت یکماه است بمرض نوبه بسیار سخت مبتلا بودم بحمدالله از توجه حضرت اجل اکرم عالی

کاملاً رفع شد لکن ضعف و نقاهت باقی است ولی حالا با قوت شدم در [illegible] روی

عاجز شدم در خدمات [illegible] غلام زاده مرحوم [illegible] هر روز در خدمت جناب

قونسول و [illegible] بانک شاهنشاهی حاضر است [illegible] این روزها قدری هوا گرم [illegible]

ثانیاً بنده این هم [illegible] هر روز در خدمات جانکاری حاضر هستم

خداوند [illegible] مرحمت [illegible] بر [illegible] مدام فرماید [illegible] امر امر مبارک حضرت اجل عالی است

[illegible]

١ نمره ٣١
٢ مورخه ٢٠ شهر شوال المکرم ١٣١٧
٣ مطابق
٤ ٢٦ شهر فبروارى ١٩٠٠
٥ تصدق حضور مبارکت شوم   اولاً ہمواره از درکاه حضرت احدّیت در خواست و
مسئلت مینماید
٦ که وجود مسعود مبارک حضرت مستطاب اجل اکرم افخم عالے روحنا فدارا از کافه
حوادث محفوظ فرماید
٧ ضمناً معروض میدارد مدت یکماه بوده بمرض نوبه بسیار سخت مبتلا بودم بحمداله
از توجه حضرت اجل اکرم عالے
٨ بکلے رفع شد کننه ننه خوب در رشت یافت نمیشود ولے حالا بے قوه شدم در پیاده
روى خیلے
٩ عاجز شدم   در خدمات قونسلخانه غلام زاده میرزا مہدى را ہر روز در خدمت
جناب
١٠ قونسول و رئیس بانك شاہنشاہى حاضر است انشا اله این روزہا قدرى ہوا کرم میشود
١١ ضمناً بلکه اسبى ہم خریده ہر روز در خدمات چاکرى حاضر باشم
١٢ خداوند ظل مرحمت را بسر جان نثار مدام فرماید   زیاده امر امر مبارک
حضرتعالے است

Specimens 1902, p. 95.

Notes

All initial حـ-forms are basically the figure of eight style. صـ-forms all lack the tooth. Final لے, if not connected, is always superposed. The diagonal stroke of کـ-forms is usually high above the upright. Three dots are almost always represented by an upside-down v. The tanvin in lines 5, 7, and 11 is two curved strokes, sometimes touching: compare the hamza in lines 5, and 10, which looks similar. را in lines 6, 9, and 12, and the زا of میرزا in line 9 show a characteristic shape of ر followed by ا. The writing in the lower right margin is illegible.

Line by line:

6: the loop of the ط of مستطاب is reduced to a tooth. The ه of فداه is lacking.

7: the conventional line above ضمنا signals a change of topic.

8: by كننه ننه the writer presumably means گنگنه or گنه گنه.

11: in هر the ه connects from below and the ر is longer than usual.

12: for the squiggle to the right of this line see Guide no. 10 and Ex. 40:6.

رستم بیک

۱۳ ربیع‌الثانی ۱۳۱۸
۹ اگست ۱۹۰۰

روز شنبه ساعت بعد از ظهر در مجلس شوری وزارت

خارجه حاضر شدم که با لغات مأمور وزارت خارجه

بروم به محلی که در عوض سالها قمع کالسکه حاجی علی اکبر رسید

ساز رفته است و با لغات چیزی مسلم نیست که چه دارد رسید

مرد را ۲ است و چه معقود شده است

١ رستم بیك ١٢ ربیع الثانی ١٣١٨ ٩ اگست ١٩٠٠
٢ روز شنبه ١٤ سه ساعت بظهر مانده در مجلس مشاوره وزارت
٣ خارجه حاضر شوید که باتفاق مامور وزارت خارجه
٤ بروید به محلی که در عرض راه قم کالسکه حاجی علی اصغر کالسکه
٥ ساز افتاده است و باتفاق یکدیکر معلوم کنید که چه از کالسکه
٦ مزبور باقی است و چه مفقود شده است

Specimens 1902, p. 139.

Notes

Many letters are reduced to slightly curved diagonal strokes of about the same size, such as روز, مانده, and وزارت in line 2. Three dots, whether for one letter or clusters, are indicated by an oval, open at the bottom: see, e.g., بیك in line 1 and شنبه in line 2.

The writing at the end of line 4 becomes thin, appears heavy at the beginning of line 5, thin at the end of this line and heavy again at the beginning of line 6, showing when the writer's pen was running out of ink and when it was dipped again in the inkwell.

Line by line:

2: the figure ١٤ appears to have been added later to clarify the date. The ج and ل of مجلس are minimized.

4: ه is written twice at the end of راه to indicate that the final consonant is pronounced: see also Exx. 6:9, 64:4, 65:3, 67:4,5.

تا ۹ شهر رجب ۱۳۱۸ بوشهر خدمت سرکار جلالتمآب اجل اکرم اعظم ...

معروض میدارد بخصوص مبلغ هشتصد تومان وجه نقد از بابت تنخواه ...

عالیجاهان سرکیس و شرکاء در سنه ماضی لغایت پسته ... از شیراز به بوشهر ...

... از بن وجه ... بطور امانت ...

در بعضی راه امانت مذبور سرقت شد ... مبلغ ... سرکار عالی ...

حیران رسیده بقیه سیصد هفتاد تومان دیگر را ... استدعا داریم ...

وجه مذبور بفرمائید که ... تاخیر ... نفرمایند ...

ملاحظه ... خواهید آورد ... ایام ...

حاجی ... محمد ...

١ بتاریخ ٩ شهر رجب سنه ١٣١٨ بوشهر خدمت سرکار جلالتمآب اجل اکرم
اعظم بالیوزکری دولت بهیه انکلیسے دامت شوکته العالے
٢ معروضمیدآرد بخصوص مبلغ هشتصد تومان وجه نقد از بابت تنخاه خالصه
٣ عالیجاهان مستر دکسن و شرکاء در سنه ماضی دربابت پسته مقرری از شیراز ببوشهر
فرستاده بودند
٤ در عرض رآه امانت مذبور سرقت شد در ماه ذی قعده مبلغ یکصد سی تومان ازین
وجه بوکیل
٥ حقیران رسیده بقیه شیشصد هفتاد تومان دیکر باقی است استدعا داریم سرکار عالے
مُطالبه
٦ وجه مذبور بفرمائید که وصول شود و زیاده برین تاخیری نیفتد یقین است در این
خصوص کمال
٧ ملاطفت بعمل خواهید آورد زیاده عرضی نیست ایام دولت و شوکت مستدام باد
٨ حاج غلامعلے حاج محمد باقر ...

Specimens 1902, p. 61.

Notes

One reader has suggested that this style of writing, with its strong horizontal lines, very long diagonals, and a certain angularity, was often used by merchants. It shows sporadic features of shekasta such as the way that **فرستاده** is written in line 3, whereas **داریم**, for example, in line 5 is written with all letters separate. In two instances, medial **ا** has a madda (**میدارد** in line 2 and **راه** in line 4). The left margin was kept straight by considerable stacking. In lines 2 and 4 the number of tumans is written in words with the siyaq figures written above (not represented in the transcription).

Line by line:

1: in **بتاریخ**, the **بتا** is small, the **ر** even smaller, and the **یخ** is quite large, with the head of the **خ** unformed. **بالیوزگری**: a consular position.

2: تنخاه is a misspelling of تنخواه.

5: the zamma of مطالبه is exaggerated.

6: the hamza of بفرمائید is exaggerated. زیاده makes sense in the context, assuming that the vertical stroke below applies to the ه: compare ساده in Ex. 53:8. The curved mark above زیاده is unexplained: could it have been added later to close the gap between ز and یاده ?

7: in زیاده, the ه turns down and the diacritical hook touches it.

8: the signatures appear to be in a different hand, and the familiar squiggle follows باقر (cf. Exx. 40, 44, 48).

V

The thirteen examples in this section, in a wide variety of twentieth-century hands from Iran, Afghanistan, and Tajikistan, are taken from Levy 1951, *Ganjina-ye Asnad*, Aini 1978, Gasanli 1983, *Afghanistan Mirror* 1992 and 1993, Khomeyni 1369, a transcription of a manuscript written in A.H. 1289, a private diary from ca. 1920, and letters from private collections.

نمونه ۱۶۵

وزارت پست و تلگراف

مصدقی

آقای عزیزم

اتفاقاً مرقومه جنابعالی را امروز بعد از انقضای وقت اداری ملاحظه
و ممکن است در اداره دیر برسد. شنبه بهر صورت محل
پیدا کردم قبل از حرکت از ملاقات شریف محظوظ
شوم. چنانچه برای ملاقات در منزل تشریف و ساعات
تلفن فرمائید برای روز یکشنبه چهارم آبان ساعت سه بعد از ظهر
فرصت برسم. مرحوم را برای ابراز احساسات
صمیمانه و مراتب تشکر تقدیم میدارد.

١ خصوصی

٢ آقای عزیزم

٣ اتفاقاً مرقومه جنابعالی را امروز بعد از انقضای وقت اداری ملاحظه

٤ و ممکن است در اداره دیر رسانده باشند بهر صورت خیلی

٥ مایل بودم قبل از حرکت از ملاقات شریف محظوظ

٦ شده باشم چنانچه برای جنابعالی در منزل خودتان وقت مساعد است

٧ تلفون فرمائید برای روز یکشنبه چهارم آبان پنج بعد از ظهر

٨ خدمت برسم - موقع را برای ابراز احساسات

٩ دوستانه و خالص انه مغتنم میشمارد مخلص

Levy 1951, p. 114.

Notes

This personal letter is written on government stationery. Many of the letter-forms in this example are very small, and some cannot be seen at all (e.g., the ق in آقای in line 2, the ن and ع of جنابعالی in lines 3 and 6, the first ی of خیلی in line 4). At the same time, some forms are larger than would be expected (e.g., the ت in اتفاقاً and the ن of انقضای in line 3, and the tooth of ص twice in line 9). Many of the intital ح-forms are figures of eight (e.g. ملاحظه in line 3). Medial ع often looks like a medial ب-form (e.g., بعد in lines 3 and 7). In spite of the hasty appearance of the writing, almost all of the dots are present. Initial م of the last three words of line 9 make an interesting study when compared with initial م in the rest of the letter.

Line by line:

3: the ی of جنابعالی is recurved and minimized: see also line 6.

4: the ه of اداره is a small loop at the end of the ر.

5: the ل of مایل and قبل does not ascend.

6: the grammar requires باشم but the form is assimilated to the common logographic form of باشد.

7: in فرمائيد the فر and ما run together and the م disappears; there is no tooth for the ى. In ظهر the loop of ظ and the hook of ه are telescoped and the upright is slightly to the left.

9: The logograph for دو in دوستانه resembles that for كه. The انه of خالصانه is minimized and superposed. The dots of the غ and ت of مغتنم are clustered. The خ of مخلص is the heavy blob at the bottom right of the ل.

تاریخ ۱۷ شهر صفر المظفر ۵ دلو مطابق ۱۳۳۱

تشخیص بده را در (مشروطان) (مشروطه) به لفظ مخصوص انگلیسی

همه بزرگ آنها خانم را دوست دارند لیکن در منزل مخصوص نه در دکان آنها

اسم کشیده در بالای نمکی مخصوص برسند

١ تاريخ ١٧ شهر صفر المظفر ٥ دلو .... مطابق ١٣٣١
٢ مستحفظين راه راور (مستر جان)(و مستر پتر) دو نفر صاحبمنصب انگليسى
٣ مهندس راه آهن عازم راور هستند البته در هر منزل مستحفظ بقدر لزوم و كفايت با آنها
٤ همراه كنيد كه سالماً بمحل مقصود برسند

Levy 1951, p. 118.

Notes

There is a tendency to write extended final letters the same: cf. مستحفظين in line 2, مهندس and آهن in line 3, and بمحل in line 4. Cf. the same tendency in Ex. 5.

Line by line:

1: the ا and ل of المظفر are connected at the top. See Guide no. 26.

2: the ا of انگليسى is written below the rest of the word (see also البته in line 3).

3: the اه of راه are written as one penstroke (also in line 2, and in همراه in line 4, where it shows most clearly). The ا of عازم is minimized.

سواد ورقه حکومت کرمانشاهان

مورخه ۳/۱۱ ماه ۵ ۱۳۱

نمره ۲۰۸۹

وزارت داخله

حکومت کرمانشاهان

محرمانه به [illegible] حکومت

مقصود از نهضت بانوان در کشور فقط این نبوده است که رفع حجاب بنمایند زیرا در کشور ایران [illegible] از

عادات زشت شمرده نشده [illegible] بوده و اکثر قرا و قصبات بهیچوجه چنین عادتی نداشته اند و این قسمت

از اقدامات [illegible] لازم است نهایت که مقصود باید بانوان حرکتی نمایند اینست که از [illegible] مختلفه

بیرون آمده و [illegible] بانوان متمدن دنیا در آیند یعنی باید لباس بلند و [illegible] و کلاههای [illegible]

[illegible] بپوشند [illegible] و جهت [illegible] پارچه و [illegible]

دارند که هر کس خواهد [illegible] از قبیل [illegible] پارچه

خارجه اجتناب نمایند و لباسهای [illegible] شایسته [illegible]

[illegible] حکمران کرمانشاهان — [illegible]

۱ سواد مراسله حکومت کرمانشاہان
۲ مورخه ۱۱-۳ ماه ۱۳۱۵
۳ نمره ۲۰۸۹
٤ متحد المال به نواب حکومت
۵ مقصود از نہضت بانوان در کشور فقط این نبوده است که رفع حجاب نمایند زیرا در
کشور ایران رو کرفتن از
٦ عادات زشت شہرنشینان بوده و اہالے قراء و قصبات بہیچوجه چنین عادتے
نداشته اند و این قسمت
۷ اقدامی که لازم است نایب الحکومه و سایر مامورین دولتی نمایند این است که لباس
از اشکال مختلفه
۸ بیرون آمده و بشکل بانوان متمدن دنیا در آیند یعنی باید لباس بلند و ساده و
کلاہہای سبك وزن
۹ بپوشند و بدیہی است طرز تہیه و قیمت لباس از حیث خوبے و بدی پارچه و دوخت به
تناسب
۱۰ دارائے ہر کسی خواہد بود که در عین حال بعموم نصیحت بدہید که از تجملات و
استعمال پارچه
۱۱ خارجه اجتناب نمایند و لباسہای فعلی آنہا نباید شبیه به لباسہای ایلاتے بوده باشد
۱۲ محل امضاء - حکمران کرمانشاهان - سواد مطابق اصل است

Ganjina-ye Asnād 1370 I, p. 15.

Notes

Line by line:

4: the first two words are underlined.

6: the kasra under the hamza has not been transcribed in قراء, and in امضاء in line 12.

7: the ل of لباس is reduced to a tooth. See also بلند in line 8.

8: ساده and کلاہہا have long hooks under the ه: there are three such long hooks in line 10 and one in line 11.

10: the ل of حال does not ascend and resembles a ن: see also استعمال.

12: the ها of كرمانشاهان is lacking.

بسیار معقول بود تر در این ایام جناب اجل امیر [illegible] قبل از این مرحوم [illegible] ملک [illegible] سلطان العلماء [illegible]

از طرف [illegible] مرحمت کرده بودند روز در منزل [illegible] ایشان تقویم و [illegible] ملاحظه توقف [illegible] جدا

طول کشید واقع رضی بمفارقت آن [illegible] شدم [illegible] از [illegible] شهر [illegible] وارد [illegible]

شده در مشهد با [illegible] و نوکر [illegible] حرکت را از [illegible] مراجعت [illegible]

دار [illegible] الآن و حکومت [illegible] دار [illegible] در [illegible] حضرت آن [illegible] و سلام در [illegible]

[illegible] عازم [illegible] شدم [illegible] از کثرت خرج و خرابی [illegible] محصور شده [illegible] اما

[illegible] آمدیم تربت [illegible] چند روزی [illegible] ملاذ العلما توقف کرده عازم [illegible]

[illegible] اطفال شدم بعد از ورود [illegible] ماه مبارک رمضان [illegible] شیخ [illegible] مرحوم [illegible] الدوله [illegible]

رفتم [illegible] عازم [illegible] بعد از یازده روز توقف [illegible]

[illegible] آمد [illegible] عروس [illegible] هزار [illegible] حکم [illegible]

[illegible] از [illegible] گرفت [illegible]

گفته که [illegible] سلطان [illegible] گفته چرا [illegible] حکم [illegible]

[illegible] السلطنه [illegible] عازم [illegible] شد [illegible]

شده که [illegible] دار [illegible] ملک و [illegible] حرکت [illegible]

[illegible] السلطنه [illegible] توقف [illegible] حکومت [illegible]

بعد از [illegible] هزار [illegible] توقف [illegible] معتمد السلطنه [illegible]

[illegible] توقف [illegible] ملک [illegible] خیال [illegible]

کردند [illegible] الصدر گفته بودند [illegible]

[illegible] معلوم [illegible] سالار [illegible] فراهم آمد [illegible]

[illegible] الصدر [illegible] نمی [illegible] از [illegible] مرحوم [illegible]

[illegible] اگرچه [illegible] بود خوش [illegible]

۱ بسیار معقولے بودند در این ایام جناب اقا میرزا محمد باقر اقا اقازاده مرحوم خلد
اشیان حاجی سلطانعلے شاه رحمة اله علیه
۲ از طهران مراجعت کرده بودند ده روز در منزل سراب باہم بودیم و چون جہة پاره
ملاحظات توقف ایشان چندان
۳ طول نکشید واقع راضی بمفارقت ایشان نبودم چاره ہم نبود از بیست (؟) ہفتم شہر
ذی حجه اقای امین التجار وارد بر حقیر
٤ شد در مشہد با اسب و نوکر الے ماه جمد الآخر که ایشان را حرکت دادم تشریف
فرما بودند بہانه این بود که مرافعه
۵ دارند با آقایان و حکومت غرض دارند بالاخره درشکه جهه ایشان خریده ایشان را
فرستادم در ماه رجب بیست شتر
٦ خریده عازم کناباد شدم الحق این است از کثیر خرج و خرابے دنباله مجبور شدم
آمدم کناباد و الا ابدا
۷ خیال کناباد نداشتم آمدیم تربت چند روزی در باغ جناب حاجی ملا علے توقف کرده
عازم کناباد با جمیع اہالے منزل
۸ خود و اطفال شدم بعد از ورود کناباد در ماه مبارک رمضان سالار اشجع پسر مرحوم
شوکه الدوله حاکم شد
۹ رفتم دیدن ایشان فردایش عازم کیسور شدم بعد از پانزده روز توقف مراجعت شد
عصری جناب حاجی معین الاشراف
۱۰ دیدن حقیر آمدند مقارن غروب امین التجار آمدند که مبلغ هزار تومان اقای حکمران
از من باسم ده یك مطالبه
۱۱ میدارند و نمی توانم تهیه وجه نمایم مبلغ سی صد تومان قرضیه از حقیر کرفت و
بردند جویمند هر که بوده دروغی بایشان
۱۲ کفته که مظفر السلطان امین التجار را کفته چرا باید چنین پولے بدہی جناب حکمران
بدون تحقیق فوری شکایت زیاد
۱۳ به ایالت عرض میکنند بیست و پنجم دستخط حضرت اقای قوام السلطنه رسید که به
دون تسامح عازم مشہد شو اسباب حیرت
۱٤ شد که بیجہه احظار حقیر چه جہة دارد ازباب اینکه موقع حاصل ملك و علاوه دو سال
سفر قوه حرکت نبود بتوسط
۱۵ جناب آقای مقبل السلطنه استدعای اجازه توقف نمود نتیجه نداد بالاخره بتوسط

حکومت وقت مخابره شد تلکراف
۱۶ بعد از مبلغ هزار دویست تومان دادن رفتن مشهد موقوف شد حقیر به کمانم اقای
مقبل السلطنه اسباب چینی کرده
۱۷ چون زمان توقف مشهد که ملك را از ایشان امنای استانه مقدسه خیال داشتند
بکیرند و مبلغ کلے اقای شجاع التولیه علاوه
۱۸ کردند ایشان تصور کرده بودند محرک حقیر بوده مدتے کله میکردند کمان میکردم
ایشان این اسباب چینی را فرموده اند
۱۹ بالاخره معلوم شداقای سالار اشجع بیجهه دشمنی کرده اسباب جهه بنده چیده
بهمین عله اسباب رنجش فراهم آمد این مدت
۲۰ قلیل (؟) حکمرانے فوق انچه تصور بود تعدی نسبت به عموم رعایا کرد از اتفاقات
بلشویك های روسیه هجوم کرده
۲۱ بودند اکرچه بعضی را عقیده این بود خرج تراشی جهه دولت فقط نظریه اقای قوام
السلطنه ... بود

Unpublished diary of Mozaffar al-Soltan, Governor of Gonabad, Khorasan, circa 1920, p. 5. From a private collection.

Notes

In lines 1, 4, 6, 7, 8 آقای is written as a logograph (see Guide no. 28). In مبلغ the ل does not rise. In lines 13 and 15 the ا of السلطنه is written below the word. There is a general tendency for the last words of a line to intrude on the line above with results that often make decipherment difficult.

Line by line:

2: the dot above بودیم is unexplained.

3: for the form of بیست, cf. the same word in line 13 below.

9: گیسور is a village some 20 miles east of Juymand (line 11) in the district of Gonabad.

10: مطالبه is difficult to distinguish from ایشان in the line below.

13: بدون is written as two separate words.

14: احظار is a misspelling of احضار. The diagonal of the ک of ملك interferes with السلطنه above.

15: بالاخره appears to have an extra ا.

17: a ۲ written above the س of مقدسه: see also Exx. 31:16, 57, 58, and Guide no. 78. The ی of آقای runs through the را of اسباب چینی را below.

عنایست بحرت سمرقند

حبذا شهر سمرقند بهشتی تمثال جز بهشتش بطراوت نتوان یافت مثال

زرنثار است زمینش چو کف اهل کرم فیض بار است هوایش چو دل اهل کمال

سبزه زاریست که هر سبزه بحیا رنگ گلاب چشمه ساریست زهر چشمه روان آب زلال

میرسد نکهت کیفیت اصحاب یمین گر وزد باد شمال از طرف باغ شمال

این سمرقند همانست که سلطان تیمور داد از این شهر باورنگ جهان زیب جلال

این سمرقند همانست الغ بیگ میرزا زد از این خطه بدانش علم استقلال

این سمرقند همانست که بولیث فقیه کرد صیت شرفش تا بحرستان اقبال

بخدا هست سمرقند خراب اوقا لیک نزد اهل سخن بحران بخارا ز خیال

گر بفردوس برندم نرود از خاطر یاد دروازه قرشی و هوای وزگاله

این همه ملک بخاراست که در عهد امیش منبع علم باسلام شده چندین سال

این همه ملک بخاراست امام اسماعیل زد از این خطه باقطار جهان کوس کمال

این همه ملک بخاراست علی سینا را رتبه داد که نادیده کسی تا این حال

١ بمناسبت ہجرت بسمرقند

٢ حبّذا شہر سمرقند بہشتی تمثال
جز بہشتش بطراوت نتوان یافت مثال

٣ زر نثار است زمینش چو کف اہل کرم
فیض بار است ہوایش چو دل اہل کمال

٤ سبزه زاری است بہر سبزه عیان رنك طرب
چشمه ساری است ز ہر چشمه روان آب زلال

٥ میرسد نکہت کیفیّت اصحاب یمین
گر وزد باد شمال از طرف باغ شمال

٦ این سمرقند ہمان است که سلطان تیمور
داد ازین شہر باورنك جہان زیب جمال

٧ این سمرقند ہمان است الغ بیك میرزا
زد ازین خِطّه بدانش علم استقلال

٨ این سمرقند ہمان است که بو لیث فقیه
کرد صیت شرفش تا عربستان ایصال

٩ غمزدای است سمرقند و طرب افزا لیك
نزداید غم ہجران بخارا ز خیال

١٠ گر بفردوس برندم نرود از خاطر
یاد دروازه قرشی و ہوای وگزال

١١ این ہمان ملك بخارا است ز جہد اہلش
منبع علم باسلام شده چندین سال

١٢ این ہمان ملك بخارا است امام اسماعیل
زد ازین خطّه با قطار جہان کوس کمال

١٣ این ہمان ملك بخارا است علی سینارا
رتبۀ داد که نا دیده کسی تا این حال

Aini 1978, p. 42.

Notes

A draft of a poem, in the author's own hand. Distinctive features include final ل, which usually has a small bowl, sometimes closed. Final ر is often greatly lengthened. There is some stacking of words and letters, possibly to accommodate the format of poetry.

Line by line:

2: something is written above تمثال.

5: the ح of اصحاب suggests a م: cf. يمين and شمال in the same line.

6: an error (تيمور سلطان) is crossed out.

از پروگرام حزب کمونیست اتحاد شوروی!

کمونیسم چیست ؟

کمونیسم عبارتست از نظام اجتماعی بدون طبقات با مالکیت واحد همگانی مردم بر وسائل تولید و برابری کامل اجتماعی همه اعضای جامعه در آن جامعه، بهمراه تکامل همه جانبه افراد نیروهای مولده نیز بر بنیاد علم و تکنیک دائماً در حال پیشرفت است راه تکامل میپیماید و کلیه سرچشمه های ثروت اجتماعی با شدت تمام فوران میزند و بدینسان اصل عالیه " از هر کس طبق استعدادش و بهر کس طبق نیازش " تحقق میپذیرد.

از پروگرام حزب کمونیست اتحاد شوروی

کمونیسم چیست ؟

کمونیسم عبارتست از نظام اجتماعی بدون طبقات با مالکیت واحد همگانی مردم بر وسائل تولید و برابری کامل اجتماعی همه اعضای جامعه که در آن جامعه بهمراه تکامل همه جانبه افراد نیروهای مولده نیز بر بنیاد علم و تکنیک که دائماً در حال پیشرفت است راه تکامل میپیماید و کلیه سرچشمه های ثروت اجتماعی با شدت تمام فوران میزند و بدینسان اصل عالیه " از هر کس طبق استعدادش و بهر کس طبق نیازش " تحقق میپذیرد

۱ از پروگرام حزب کمونیست اتحاد شوروی !
۲ کمونیسم چیست؟
۳ کمونیسم عبارتست از نظام اجتماعی بدون طبقات با مالکیت واحد
٤ ہمگانی مردم بر وسائل تولید و برابری کامل اجتماعی ہمه اعضای
۵ جامعه که در ان جامعه ، بهمراه تکامل ہمه جانبه افراد
٦ نیروهای مولده نیز بر بنیاد علم و تکنیکی که دائماً در حال پیشرفت است
۷ راه تکامل میپیماید و کلیه سر چشمه های ثروت اجتماعی با شدت
۸ تمام فوران میزند و بدینسان اصل عالیه از هر کس
۹ طبق استعدادش و بهر کس طبق نیازش
۱۰ تحقق میپذیرد .

Gasanli 1983, pp. 10–11.

Notes

The shekasta version on the right, transcribed here, comes with its own transcription in nasta‘liq on the left. The two samples differ slightly in wording and line length: for example, in line 6 of the nasta‘liq version a small ی is written in parentheses above the final ک of تکنیك, and a very small دائماً is written above که.

There are inconsistencies in the shekasta style: cf. the ligature اد in lines 1 and 5, and the change in the form of initial ه after line 5.

Final ی is extended (except for one instance in line 4). Final ن is sometimes recurved. Initial ا has a serif. The left end of final ت curves up sharply, and groups of three dots are usually written as a circle. د is generally exaggerated; see Guide no. 35. Modern punctuation such as a comma (line 5), a question mark (line 2), quotation marks (lines 8–9), and an exclamation point (line 1) is used. The quotation marks are not represented in the transcription.

Line by line:

2: The three dots of چ are written under the س of کمونیسم (which is written in nasta'liq, probably for emphasis).

3: in عبارتست the final ت is not joined to the preceding س.

4: for مردم see Guide no. 44.

6: there is an unusual ligature of رو in نیروها (see Guide no. 44), and of ال in حال.

7: the head of چ in چشمه ها, is a figure of eight form, and the circle representing the dots of ث in ثروت is written over the tail of the ی from the line above.

9: the second د of استعداد is missing.

باستان شناسان افغان - شوروی پس از کاوش ها در حویات زرتشتی مقبره طلاتپه در سال ۱۹۷۸ عیسوی تعداد بیست هزار توته طلا که قدامت آنرا دو هزار سال قبل تخمین نموده اند کشف کردند.

باستان شناسان (آرکیالوجست) شوروی قبلاً در سال ۱۹۶۹ بخاطر کاوش ها و تحقیقات نواحی باکتریا (بلخ) که مرکز راه ابریشم بود آمده بودند.

در ناحیه شمال افغانستان، در شهر شبرغان برآمدگی موسوم به طلاتپه با قبرهای پر از طلا و جواهرات توسط باستان شناسان کشف گردیده که اموات با طلا و جواهرات دفن شده که دیدن آنها چشم را خیره میسازد.

آثار و غنایم (آرتی فکتس) شامل طلای خالص و جواهرات قیمت بها و همچنان بعضی احجار نیمه لذرش را شامل بوده که باستان شناسان نمیتوانند این اندوخته قدیمی را به قیمت ارزیابی نمایند و دنیا گفته ها که بالاتر از قیمت قیمت ها میباشند.

طوریکه آنهم باختران چهار هزار سال قبل از نعمت حکومت های مستقل برخوردار بوده و دوره‌های دول در تحت تأثیر امپراطوری ها توسط طلب همسایه دیگر همسایه قرار گرفته اند.

۱ باستان شناسان افغان - شوروی پس از کاوش ہا و حفریات از شش مقبره طلا تپه در سال
۲ ۱۹۷۸ عیسوی مقدار بیست ہزار توته طلا که قدامت آنرا دو ہزار سال قبل تخمین
۳ نموده اند کشف کردند .
٤ باستان شناسان (آرکیالوجست) شوروی قبلاً در سال ۱۹٦۹ بخاطر کاوش ها و تحقیقات
۵ نواحی باکتریا (بلخ) که مرکز راه ابریشم بود آمده بودند .
٦ در ناحیه شمال افغانستان ، در شہر شبرغان بر آمدگی موسم به طلا تپه با قبر ہای پُر از طلا
۷ و جواهرات توسط باستان شناسان کشف گردیده که اموات با طلا و جواهرات
۸ دفن شده که دیدن آنہا چشم ہارا خیره میسازد .
۹ آثار و غنایم (آرتی فکتز) شامل طلای خالص و جواهرات قیمت بہا و همچنان
۱۰ بعض احجار نیمه ارزش را شامل بوده که باستان شناسان نمیتوانند این اندوخته قدیمی
۱۱ را به قیم ارزیابی نمایند ؛ و بنا به گفته ہا که بالاتر از قیمت قیمت ها میباشند .
۱۲ طوری که آگاهیم باختریان چہار هزار سال قبل از نعمت حکومت ہای مستقل بر خوردار بوده
۱۳ و در پای قرون در تحت تأثیر امپراطوری های توسعه طلب همسایه و غیر همسایه قرار
۱٤ گرفته اند .

Afghanistan Mirror June–July, 1992 III, p. 121.

Notes

In this and the following example the small size of the writing plus considerable minimization create special problems. The most important usage common to both examples is a mark resembling a small numeral **۳** often written above a toothless **س**: see also Exx. 31:16, 54:17, 58, and Guide no. 78. Separate **ها**

is written in a variety of styles in this example but the following example (Ex. 58) from the same source is quite consistent in using one form.

Line by line

1: پس and سال have a mark above the س which is probably a reduced form of the small ۳ mentioned above. Note the variant renderings of ها of کاوش ها here and in line 4.

2: note the small ۳ above the س of بیست. The ه of هزار (twice; also in line 12) is written in its full form but also has a hook below. توته: piece.

4: note the small ۳ above the س of آرکیالوجست.

5: the ه of راه is superposed.

6: the ه of شهر is minimized. موسم is an error for موسوم.

8: note the variant renderings of ها in آنها and چشم ها.

9: the ی of قیمت lacks a tooth and can be identified only from its dots. The end of the ت of the same word curves up to meet the two dots.

10: note the difference between the ش of شامل here and in line 9.

11: a semi-colon is used after نمایند.

12: the ی of باختریان is visible only by its dots. The ه of چهار has a hook below.

کمونیست های پیرو ماسکو:

در دوران صدارت محمد داود خان مرحوم عطش پشتونستان طلبی و نزدیکی مناسبات شوروی و افغانستان مساعدترین زمینه را برای پرورش جوجه‌های لنینی در کشور فراهم کرد. نفوذ در معارف اولین پایگاه این میکروب های "ام الفساد" به اردو و ادارات ملکی سرایت کرد. در دهه قانون اساسی جوجه‌ها که تازه از تخم سر به در کرده بودند، افتان و خیزان به راه افتادند و به حیث جاسوس‌های ماهر دور سفارت شوروی حلقه زدند. قوت دانه و دام جوجه‌ها را به سرعت پرورانید و بنام حزب "دیموکراتیک خلق" سازماندهی کرد. سفارت شوروی آنها را در دو کاسه نان داد یکی در کاسه پشتون خواهان خلقی از برای حمایت پشتونستان طلبی و دیگر در کاسه حکومت یاران پرچمی تا در درون حکومت و دفتر مجریان امور نفوذ نمایند، بی‌خبر از آنکه نوزادی جدید از این پیوند بنام ستمی‌های غیرپشتون نیز پیدا خواهد شد.

١ کمونیست های پیرو ماسکو :

٢ در دوران صدارت محمد داود خان مرحوم عطش پشتونستان طلبی و نزدیکی مناسبات شوروی و افغانستان مساعدترین زمینه

٣ را برای پرورش چوچگان لنین در کشور فراهم کرد . نفوذ در معارف اولین پایگاه این میکروب بود که بعداً به اردو

٤ و ادارات ملکی سرایت کرد . در دهه قانون اساسی چوچه ها که تازه از تخم سر بدر کرده بودند ،افتان و خیزان

٥ به راه افتادند و به حیث جایگاه مادر دور سفارت شوروی حلقه زدند . قوت دانه و دام چوچه ها را به سرعت

٦ پرورانید و بنام حزب دیموکراتیك خلق سازماندهی کرد . سفارت شوروی آنها را در دو کاسه نان داد

٧ یکی در کاسه پشتون خواهان خلقی از برای حمایت پشتونستان طلبی و دیگر در کاسه حکومت یاران پرچمی تا

٨ در داخل حکومت و قشر مجریان امور نفوذ نمایند ،بی خبر از آنکه نوده ای جدید از این پیوند بنام ستمی های

٩ غیر پشتون نیز بعداً خواهد روئید .

Afghanistan Mirror IV April–May, 1993, p. 35.

Notes

See the general notes for the previous example. Three dots below a letter (پ ، چ, etc.) are often written as a zig-zag.

Line by line:

2: in خان, the ن is a superposed continuation of the ا.

3: the form of بود is noteworthy for the way in which ب and و connect: see also بودند in line 4.

6: the quotation marks around دیموکراتیك خلق are not represented in the transcription.

شهرها بر مدینه و تحکیلات و زراعت دارد هر شهری موسوم به اسمی می‌باشد و بعضی از آن مزارع قلعه مبنی کرده باشند

و برج متعدد ساخته‌اند که دوازده قلعه از قلاع معروف آن عرض می‌شود اول لنگر دوم آبشار سیم

ایراقشان چهارم سربانه پنجم ذوب ششم کوی هفتم کشتی هشتم اصول کان نهم

پارو دهم فیروزآباد یازدهم بقان دوازدهم هشابون فصل بیان رود هیرمند که

در چند جا در تفصیل او در فصل‌ها این سواد قلم شده جمع می‌شود و مصرف شرب اهالی آن‌ها می‌رسد و هلمند الکم

با ترکه روز بعد از کوه اشپ بحث کنیم آن‌ها حاصل می‌شود اشکسته حمل از زیر تحکیلات دیگر دست زیر رود عات

است خبر که غلیظ و عفن است محصول آن‌ها گندم و جو و ذرت و باقلا و دیگر دهات است معامل چهار پر دور از آن

عمل می‌آید و بیش کرده چیزها محصول و بعضی از اجناس آن‌ها با یکدیگر داد و ستد می‌کنند و کیح منزه و به ایجاد چهار نیز می‌کند

عدد نفوس سکنه آن‌ها جمیعا هزار بیست و بیست که گفته شد تقریبا ده هزار نفر جنگی دارد و زبان‌شان بلوچی می‌باشد

مذهب‌شان بعضی سنی و [illegible] برخی اسماعیلی ذکری گویند این ذکری شریعت شیعه و سنی عمل نمی‌کنند

١ نهر ها بریدند و نخیلات و زراعت دارد هر نهری موسوم باسمی میباشد در بعضی از
آن مزارع قلعه مبنی بر حصار بلند

٢ و بروج متعدد ساختند دوازده قلعه از قلاع معروف آنجا عرض میشود اول
نسکند ، دیم آشار سیم

٣ ایر افشان چهارم سرباز پنجم دُوْپ ششم کور هفتم کشی هشتم اصول کان نهم

٤ پارود دهم فیروزاباد یازدهم بافتان دوازدهم هُشابُون فاضلاب این رود میرود بجدکال

٥ در خندقے که تفصیل او در فصل تالے این مسوده قلمی شده جمع میشود و بمصرف
شرب اهالے انجا میرسد هوای انجا کرم است

٦ پانزده روز بعد از تحویل آفتاب بحمل کندم آنجا حصد میشود ابش پیوسته چون از زیر
نخیلات و برنج و سایر مزروعات

٧ است جزئے غلیظ و عفن است محصول انجا کندم و جو و زرت و باقلا و برنج و ماش
است سالے معادل چهار کرور از این اجناس

٨ عمل می آید و شش کرور خرما میشود خرما و بعضی از اجناس آنجا را بجدکال و
دشتیاری و کیچ میبرند و به بندر چابهار نیز می برند

٩ عدد نفوس سکنه آنجا چهل هزار متجاوز است که تقریباً ده هزار مرد جنگلی دارد
زبانشان بلوچی میباشد

١٠ مذهبشان بعضی سنّی و برخی را ذکری گویند این ذکری ها شریعت شیعه و سنّی عمل
نمیکنند

در بیرون هر یکی از دهات خودشان مسجدی دارند که بنده فقیر دیده‌ام چه اگر مرد و زن آنها جمع می‌شوند و معتقد او می‌شد

آن زنان با مردان وصلت شدند ذکر می‌کنند تا بر او عشق و بیهشی طاری می‌شود در آنوقت هر زن بخت بر گردد وقتی که با او جمع می‌شود

وصلت شده‌اند گویند بعضی از زنهای آنها خوش‌سیما و مقبوله‌اند حیوانات بارکش و سواری مردم اینجا بیشتر شتر است که گوسفند

زیادی دارند پشم و کرک آنها به بندر چابهار و سیر باهند قریب به آنجا می‌برند گراز در دهات و جنگلها بسیار

سالاریان از جزایر کراز البتوه می‌آیند و همیشه شکایت دارند در جنگل قهستان آنجا که گوسفند کوهی بسیار و ... شد صید

صید می‌نمایند شغل سکنه آنجا بیشتر قلندری و چوپانی است آنجا از زراعات و جمعها و ... آنجا

در کوه آنجا معدن ... مشهور است الیکن ... معمور راه عراده از ... تا ... و از آنجا بیشتر به بندر چابهار

هر چه وجه تسمیه سرباز به تحقیق معلوم نشد از اصول مشکونه فی جوف الارض چنین ... سرباز

آورده عمل می‌آید در همه جا این اصول مشکونه فی جوف الارض اگر رغبت کنند عمل خواهد آمد چنین مگو آنجا

کم شعور و بی‌سلیقه و آبادانی ندیده‌اند اهتمام در عمل آوردن آنها ندارند بلکه بعضی به هیچ‌وجه نمی‌شناسند

١١ در ہر دھی از دھات خودشان مسجدی دارند سالے یکدفعه در آن مساجد اکثر مرد و زن آنہا جمع میشوند و مقتدا و مرشد

١٢ آنہا بزبان بلوچی و صدای بلند ذکر می کند تا بر او غش و بیہُشی طاری میشود در انوقت ہر زن بدست ہر مرد افتاد با او جمع میشود

١٣ و حلال میداند کویند بعضی از زنہای آنہا خوش سیما و مقبوله اند حیوان بارکش و سواری مردم آنجا بیشتر شتر است کوسفند

١٤ زیاد دارند پشم و کورک آنہا به بندر چابہار و سایر بنادر قریب بانجا میبرند کراز در رودخانه و جنکل آنجا زیاد است

١٥ زارعین از خرابے کراز بستوه می آیند و پیوسته شکایت دارند در قلال قہستان انجا کوسفند کوھی میباشد و صیادان

١٦ صید مینمایند شغل سکنه آنجا بیشتر فلاحی و جولاھی است مالیات انجا از مزروعات و خرما ده من دو من است

١٧ در کوه آنجا معدن سرب میباشد که اکنون ہم معمور است راه عراده از بمپور بانجا میباشد و از انجا نیز به بندر چابہار

١٨ میرود وجه تسمیه سرباز بتحقیق معلوم نشد از اصول متکونه فے جوف الارض ، چغندر و پیاز

١٩ در آنجا عمل می آید در همه بلوچستان این اصول متکونه فے جوف الارض اگر زراعت کنند عمل خواہد آمد چون مردم انجا

٢٠ کم شعور و بے سلیقه و آبادانے ندیده اند اهتمام در عمل آوردن آنہا ندارند بلکه بعضی را بہیچوجه نمی شناسند

From a transcription made in 1967 of a manuscript on the history and geography of the Baluch from the library of Amir Tavakkol Kambuzia, written in 1289.

Notes

The toponym چاه بهار is consistently spelled چابهار. The following is a list of the toponyms in mentioned in this example: آشار ، اصول کان ، ایر افشان بافتان ، بمپور ، پارود ، جدگال ، چاه بهار ، دشتیاری ، دوپ ، سرباز ، فیروزاباد ، کشی ،کور ،کیچ ،نسکند ،هشابون .

Line by line:

2: there are two unexplained lines above نسکند.

3: ایر: lower. There is an unexplained mark above کور.

2–4: this is a list of places with forts.

4: a small unexplained mark appears parallel to the upper part of the ا in فیروزاباد and هشابون.

بسمه تعالی

جناب حجت الاسلام آقای شیخ محمدعلی انصاری دامت افاضاته

جنابعالی که فردی متدین و آگاه می باشید به عنوان نماینده اینجانب با دو نفر از طرف شورای محترم نگهبان دیگر
و دو نفر از طرف وزیر محترم کشور موظف می باشید تا با بررسی دقیق مسائل مربوطه کار انتخابات تهران را به پایان
برسانید ۱- آقایان باید تمام تلاش خود را بنمایند تا انتخابات مرحله دوم در روز قبلی صورت گیرد و مجلس
سوم در وقت مقرر تشکیل گردد. ۲- هیئت نظارت شورای محترم نگهبان موظف است که از ابتدا تعداد
صندوقهایی را که از آنها شکایت شده است مشخص نماید ۳- وزارت کشور موظف است تمامی صندوقهای مورد
شکایت را هم امروز به شورای محترم نگهبان منتقل گرداند. ۴- وزارت کشور می تواند افرادی را در موقع شمارش
آرا بر سر صندوقها بگمارد تا برای هیچکس هیچ شبهه ای پیش نیاید ۵- آرا نسبت به کاندیداها شمارش شود نه
کاندیداهای خاص. مسئولیت حفظ صندوقهای منتقل شده با شورای نگهبان است. جنابعالی موظف می باشید تا
مسائل را به اینجانب گزارش نمایید تا قوه قضائیه با هر کس که در راه پیشبرد کار مانع ایجاد می کند قاطعانه
برخورد نماید. خداوند همه را به راه راست هدایت فرماید و از کید شیطان نفس نجات دهد

والسلام خمینی

[illegible]

١ بسمه تعالے
٢ جناب حجة الاسلام آقای حاج شیخ محمد علی انصاری دامت افاضاته
٣ جنابعالے که فردی متدین و آکاه می باشید بعنوان نماینده اینجانب با دو نفر از طرف
شورای محترم نگهبان
٤ و دو نفر از طرف وزیر محترم کشور موظف می باشید تا بموارد ذیل عمل نموده و کار
انتخابات تهران را به پایان
٥ برسانید ١ - آقایان باید تمام تلاش خودرا بنمایند تا انتخابات مرحله دوّم در روز
قدس صورت گیرد و مجلس
٦ سوّم در وقت مقرر تشگیل گردد . ٢ - هیئت نظارت شورای محترم نگهبان موظف
است که از ابتدا تعداد
٧ صندوقهائی را که از آنها شکایت شده است مشخص نمایند ٣ - وزارت کشور موظف
است تمامی صندوقهای مورد
٨ شکایت را هم امروز بشورای محترم نگهبان منتقل گرداند . ٤ - وزارت کشور می
تواند افرادی را در موقع شمارش
٩ آرا بر سر صندوقها بگمارد تا برای مجلس هیچ شبهه ای پیش نیاید ٥ - آرا ، نسبت
بهمه کاندیداها شمارش شود نه
١٠ کاندیداهای خاص . مسئولیت حفظ صندوقهای منتقل شده با شورای نگهبان است .
جنابعالے موظف می باشد تا
١١ مسائل را به اینجانب گزارش نمائید تا قوه قضائیه با هر کس که در راه پیشبرد کار
های مانع ایجاد می کنند قاطعانه
١٢ بر خورد نماید خداوند همه را براه راست هدایت فرماید و از کید شیطان نفس
نجات دهد و السلام
١٣ روح اله الموسوی الخمینی

Khomeyni 1369 XX, p. 203.

Notes

A letter written in 1367. Some letters, especially medial ـبـ-forms, and the ف of موظف are minimized.

به توللی

نظر بنده این است فیلمهایی که نمایش داده میشود همگی تقریباً ابتذال ترویج

میکند و بسیاری از فیلمها آموزنده است و بخش از آنها نیز [illegible]

همینطور فیلمهای ویدئویی

قرار دارد و همینطور [illegible] اگر اینها مبتذل است کار هر فرد

میطلبد و دیده میشود که باید بیشتر مراقبت کرد

لکن در دو [illegible] باید مراقبت شود اول کسانی

که کار را میکنند باید محترم باشند و [illegible]

چنین کارهایی را انجام دهند و دوم [illegible] [illegible]

از ورود شهوات نظر کنند

[illegible]

بسمه تعالے
نظر نمودن به این قبیل فیلمها و نمایش نامه ها مرا هیچیك اشكال شرعی
ندارد و بسیاری از انها اموزنده است و پخش انها نیز اشكالے
ندارد و همینطور فیلمهای ورزشی و همینطور اهنکها اکثرآ بے اشکال است کاهی خلاف
بطور نادر دیده میشود که باید بیشتر مواظبت کرد
لکن دو نکته باید مراعات شود اول انکه کسانے
که کریم میکنند باید محرم باشند و اجنبی حرام است
چنین کاری را انجام دهد   دوم انکه بینندکان
از روی شهوت نظر نکنند   روح اله موسوی الخمینی

Khomeyni 1369 XX, p. 167.

Notes

In this example, apparently written with a felt-tipped pen, س and ش can become indistinguishable from initial or medial ب-forms: e.g., اشكال or شرعی in line 2. All examples of آ lack the madda. Final ی varies freely among normal (شرعی in line 2), recurved (اشكالے in line 3), and extended (بسیاری in line 3). Initial ا is often written below the word. ک and گ are not distinguished. The diagonal of ک in اشكال in lines 2, 3, and 4 is vertical.

Line by line:

2: the ل of قبیل does not ascend and resembles a final ت-form. نامه ها is written with three penstrokes, one above the other. The ک of هیچیك meets the ا of اشكال. The ع of شرعی is a closed blob.

3: the ش of پخش is extended and very flat.

7: گریم: from the French *grimer*, to apply makeup to another.

9: the conventional terminating squiggle appears before the signature. See Guide no. 10.

۴۸/۱۱/۱۵

قربانت مادر

دختر عزیزم پس از عرض سلام امیدوارم که وجود عزیزت در کمال صحت

و سلامت بوده باشد اگر جویای حالات خواسته باشی الحمدالله

سلامتی حاصل است بغیر از دوری شما مدتی هم بیمار بیشترش اینجا بود

با کسی را برداشت نوشت من هم برای شوهرش نامه را نوشتم که

تو اول فکر کن حال چه شکل است بعد ببین که دختر عزیزم بابا بیا چطور

اینجا تحصیل است تازه نامه نوشتم - عزیزم محمد حسین کارنامه اش را گرفته

است همه نمره هایش ۱۵ - ۱۶ بابا سه فقط هندسه ۹ شده است خوب

بابا سلام عزیز را از خانم حالا نیز از دیروز تعطیل خوابیده است

دیگر سلام مخصوص دارند همه سلام دارند و دیده بوسی بابا

قربانت [illegible]

١ ١٥،١١،٤٨
٢ قربانت مادرت
٣ دختر عزیزم   پس از عرض سلام امیدوارم که وجود عزیزت در کمال صحت
٤ و سلامت بوده باشد اگر جویای حال من و فامیل خواسته باشی الحمد اله
٥ سلامتی حاصل است بغیر از دوری شما مهربانم نهار هوشنگ اینجا بود
٦ پاکت را ور داشت نوشت من هم برای شوخی این نامه را نوشتم که
٧ تو اول فکر کنی مال هوشنگ است بعد ببینی که دختر عزیزم میباشد چون
٨ اینجا تفصیل نیست تازه نامه نوشتم - عزیزم محمد حسین کارنامه اش را
گرفته
٩ است همه نمره هایش ١٥ - ١٦ میباشد فقط هندسه ٩ شده است خوب
١٠ میباشد عزیزتر از جانم حالا نیز از دیروز مریض خوابیده است
١١ و بتو سلام مخصوص دارند همه سلام دارند و دیده بوس میباشد
١٢ قربانت صد هزار بار نصرت شهریاری

A letter from a private collection.

Notes

Particular forms: The combinations جو, چو, and خو in وجود, جویای, خواسته, چون, خوب, and خوابیده all suppress the loop of the و. The شد of میباشد in lines 7, 9, 10, and 11 has the د terminating in an upward hook which continues up to form an almost-closed circle representing the three dots. Much the same form can be seen in باشی in line 4. There is a slight break in the upward curve in باشد in the same line, and in شما in line 5, where the sign for three dots seems to be repeated. The wavy line across the bottom of the page is on the writing paper.

Line by line:

4: الحمد اله is a common error for الحمد لله.

8: the ل of تفصیل does not ascend.

9: it is common practice to draw a line under a numeral.

11: the grammar requires میباشند, but the form is identical to میباشد in lines 7, 9, and 10.

12: the terminating squiggle begins with the final ی of شهریاری.

فیلادلفیا شانزدهم سپتامبر 1987

خواهر عزیزم ژاله جان

نامه‌ات همگی در پی وحشت زلزله آمد که [illegible] و ما [illegible] نوشته‌ام
فردا نامه برادرم نوشته بودی که بدستم رسید. میدانم که سخت است دوری عزیزان
به خصوص پدر و مادر. از این غم الکن [illegible] صدمه دیدید. بنابراین سخت
برای ما هم. من در غم اولاد شان [illegible]. این غمی است که جایش
باقی است، بر [illegible] آن خاطری نابودیست
[illegible] دوباره به [illegible] آمد، موقع مشاهده [illegible] تا هم پیشم
امید است که در دیدار آینده از [illegible] رهایی [illegible] از خجالت و دوری‌تان
نیز دیدن میسر بود. حالا هم [illegible] آواره، در هر صورت ایشان [illegible]
میسر می‌شود که با همه عزیزان گه‌گاهی در تماس باشم. لطفاً [illegible] و اقوام
دور و بر، من جان و همه را به پدر و مادر [illegible] همچنان به
صحت [illegible] و [illegible].
[illegible] که تا حال [illegible] چندین [illegible] به ایشان [illegible] بودند و [illegible]
از قضا [illegible] در تماس دیگری [illegible] هم با ایشان [illegible].

تا دیدار آینده خدا نگهدار همه‌تان

دوستتان [signature]

جمعه شب [illegible]

[illegible] در آن [illegible] در حقیقت [illegible] بودی، نامه هفته اول [illegible] از [illegible]
خدا کند که کدام جمله [illegible] زود [illegible] نشده باشد.

١ فریبورگ شانزدهم دسامبر 1987
٢ خواهرم عزیزم راحله جان
٣ مکتوب همدردی و غم شریکے ات که به تعقیب وفات جگرگوشه ام
٤ فرید نامرادم نوشته بودی برایم رسید . میدانم که خودت و سایر عزیزان
٥ به حیث پدر و یا مادر از ین غم المناک من صدمه دیدید . دعا می کنم که نه
٦ به شما و نه من دیگر غم اولاد نشان ندهد . این غم است که تا حیات
٧ باقی است ، شعله های آن خاموشی ناپذیر است .
٨ بدبختانه دو باریکه به نیو یارک آمدم ، موقع مساعد نشد که با هم بے بینیم
٩ امید است که در دیدار آینده از بچه کاکای مهربان ، از خودت و نور چشمان
١٠ نیز دیدن میسر گردد . حالا همهٔ ما آواره در هر نقطه جهان ، وقت را
١١ میسر نمی شود که با همهٔ عزیزان گاه گاهی در تماس باشیم . لطفاً محبت و
احترامات
١٢ ژورژت ، من ، احسان و هیلی را به پدر و مادرت میرسانی همچنان به
١٣ حسینه جان و ننگلی جان .
١٤ نمیدانم که تا حال عادله جان و افندی جان به پاکستان تشریف بردند و یا نه
١٥ اگر تصادفاً در تماس می شوی احترامات همه ما را میرسانی .
١٦ تا دیدار آینده خدا حافظ و ناصر همهٔ تان
١٧ دوست تان ...
١٨ مکرر اینکه ؛ در آدرسیکه در عقب نامه نوشته بودی ، نامهٔ هذا ارسال گردید . اگر
غلط نکنم به فکرم ناقص نرسید
١٩ خدا کند که کدام جمله و یا عدد از نزدت فراموش نشده باشد .

A letter from a private collection.

Notes

The principal characteristic of this hand is an extreme degree of minimization. The diagonals of ک and گ, and the madda of ا are usually quite separate from the upright. Letters and sequences of words are often widely spaced.

Although difficult to read, all individual peculiarities have been amply treated in connection with other Examples. Original reduced 5%.

Line by line:

4: for خودت see also line 9.

5: the می is written separately in میکنم.

18: نامه is written small above عقب, probably a correction.

VI

The following thirteen examples in Urdu are from the early nineteenth to the late twentieth century.

The historical ه has been differentiated into two letters. Today aspirated consonants are distinguished from unaspirated ones by the addition of ھ. In all other instances ه is used. The convention of using ھ to indicate aspirated consonants and ه to indcate the consonant *h* did not become established until the late nineteenth century. Even today the aspirated counterparts of ل ، م ، ن are most frequently written with ه, as in انہیں ، تمہیں, دلہن ، although these may also be written دلھن ، انھیں ، تمھیں.

In many of the examples that follow, ya-ye majhul is not distinguished from ya-ye ma'ruf; the three long vowels *i, e, ai* are all represented by ی.

The convention of indicating final nasal vowels by an undotted *nun* did not become widely accepted until the early 20th century. In many of our examples final nasal vowels are indicated by ن.

The pronouns اس and ان are often written اوس and اون (the addition of و or ی to indicate *pesh* or *zer* is called اعراب بالحرف). ک and گ, ج and چ, and ب and پ are not always distinguished. Medial ه often lacks its lower hook. Hamza and tashdid are inconsistently supplied.

The examples in this group are taken from Barker 1977, a manuscript dated A.H. 1247, Ghalib 1969, Muhammad Tahir 1289, 'Ashiq 1879, Chandar 1966, Siddiqui 1941, and Abu al-Hasan 1891, and letters and documents from private collections.

مجنون کو جو اسطرح سی دیکہا — نوفل کی تئیں ہوا ابریکہا

پرسش کی اوسکی داستانکی — برتاب ہوئی اوسی بیان کی

ہرچند کیا خطاب اوسنی — لیکن ندیا جواب اوسنی

آخر پوچہا کسی سی تو تنگ — کسکی لئی ہی یہہ اتنا بی ننگ

جو اوسکو خبر نہین بدنکی — جامہ کی طمع نہی کفن کی

١	مجنون کو جو اسطرحسی دیکھا	نوفل کی تئین ہوا پریکھا
٢	پرسش کي اوسکي داستانکي	پر تاب نہوئ اوسی بیان کي
٣	هر چند کیا خطاب اوسني	لیکن ندیا جواب اوسني
٤	آخر پوچھا کسی سی ہو تنگ	کسکی لئی ہی یہہ اتنا بی ننگ
٥	جو اوسکو خبر نہین بدنکی	جامه کی طمع نَہَیْ کفں کي

Barker et al. 1977, vol. 1, p. 164. From a manuscript of *Laylá wa majnun* by Mirza Muhammad Taqi Khan Hawas. The undated manuscript is attributed to the early years of the reign of Nawab Sa'adat 'Ali Khan (reg. 1798–1814) in Lucknow.

Notes

Line by line:

1: اس طرح سے are run together.

2: نه ہوئ are run together, eliding the ه of نه.

3: نه دیا are run together.

4: final aspiration is indicated for یه by writing ه twice; see also Exx. 6:9, 49:4, 65:3, 67:4,5.

5: نه ہے are run together. The ں of کفں lacks a dot.

بسم اللہ الرحمن الرحیم

کروں پہلے توحید یزداں رقم　　جھکا جس کی سجدہ میں اول قلم

سر لوح پر رکھہ بیاض جبیں　　کہا دوسرا کوئی تجھہ سا نہیں

قلم پھر شہادت کی انگلی اٹھا　　ہوا حرف زن یوں کہ رب العلا

نہیں کوئی تیرا نہو کا شریک　　تیری ذات ہی وحدہ لا شریک

پرستش کی قابل ہی تو ای کریم　　کہ ہی ذات تیری غفور الرحیم

رہی حمد میں تیرے لکھا عز و جل　　تجھی سجدہ کرتا چلوں سر کے بل

وہ الحق کہ ایسا ہی معبود ہی　　قلم جو لکھی اس سے افزود ہی

سبحانہ

١ بسم الله الرحمن الرحيم

٢ کرون پہلے توحيد يزدان رقم　　جهکا جسکی سجديمين اول قلم

٣ سر لوح پر رکهه بياض جبين　　کها دوسرا کوئی تجهه سا نہين

٤ قلم پهر شہادت کی انکلی اٹها　　ہوا حرف زن يون که رب الغلا

٥ نہين کوئی تيرا نہوکا شريك　　تيری ذات ہی وحده لاشريك

٦ پرستش کی قابل ہی تو ای کريم　　که هی ذات تيری غفور الرحيم

٧ رہی حمد مين تيرے اے عز و جل　　تجهی سجده کرتا چلون سر کے بل

٨ وه الحق که ايسا ہی معبود ہی　　قلم جو لکهی اس سے افزود هی

٩ سبہونکا

Ghulam Hamadani Mushafi, *Bahr-i muhabbat*. From a manuscript dated A.H. 1247.

Notes

Aspiration is indicated by either ه or ھ (compare جہکا in line 2 and رکہه in line 3 with تجهی in line 7 and لکهی in line 8). Final aspiration is indicated by writing ه twice (e.g., line 3; see also Exx. 6:9, 49:4, 64:4, 67:4,5).

Line by line:

2: the ح of توحيد is minimized.

4: the ٹ in اٹها is marked by four dots, a conventional practice of the time.

7: the smudge on اے results from a damaged spot in the manuscript.

8: the dot above معبود is unexplained.

9: the words سبہونکا are catchwords (tark) that anticipate the first words of the following page so that a reader can be sure that no leaf is missing in a text with unnumbered pages: see also Ex. 69:17.

پھر شوق کر رہا ہی خریدار کی طلب
عرض متاع عقل و دل و جان کیی ہوی

دوڑی ہی پھر ہر ایک گل و لالہ پر خیال
صد گلستان نگاہ کا سامان کیی ہوی

پھر چاہتا ہون نامہ دلدار کہولنا
جان نذر دلفریبی عنوان کیی ہوی

ڈہونڈی ہی پھر کسو کو لب بام پر ہوس
زلف سیاہ رخ پہ پریشان کیی ہوی

مانگی ہی پھر کسو کو مقابلمین آرزو
سرمی سی تیز دشنہ مژگان کیی ہوی

ایک نوبہار ناز کو چاہی ہی پھر نگاہ
چہرہ فروغ می سی گلستان کیی ہوی

جی ڈہونڈتا ہی پھر وہی فرصت کہ رات دن
بیٹھی رہین تصور جانان کیی ہوی

پھر دلمین ہی کہ در پہ کسو کی پڑی رہین
سر زیر بار منت دربان کیی ہوی

غالب ہمین نہ چھیڑ کہ پھر جوش اشک سے
بیٹھی ہین ہم تہیہ طوفان کیی ہوے

دیکھتا ہون وحشت شوق خروش آمادہ سے
فال رسوائی سرشک سر بصحرا دادہ سے

١ پہر شوق کر رہا ہی خریدار كي طلب   عرض متاع عقل و دل و جان کئی ہوئی
٢ دوڑی ہی پہر ہر ایك کل و لاله پر خیال   صد کلستان نکاه کا سامان کئی ہوئی
٣ پہر چاہتا ہون نامه دلدار کہولنا   جان نذر دلفریبی عنوان کئی ہوئی
٤ دہونڈہی ہی پہر کسو کو لب بام بر ہوس   زلف سیاه رخپه پریشان کئی ہوئی
٥ مانکی ہی پہر کسو کو مقابلمین آرزو   سرمی سی تیز دشنۂ مژکان کئی ہوئی
٦ ایك نو بہار ناز کو چاہی ہی پہر نکاه   چہره فروغ می سی کلستان کئی ہوئی
٧ جی دہونڈہتا ہی پہر وہی فرصت که رات دن   بیٹہی رہین تصور جانان کئی ہوئی
٨ پہر دلمین ہی که در په کسو کی پڑی رہین   سر زیر بار منت دربان کئی ہوئی
٩ غالب ہمین نچہیڑ که پہر جوش اشك سے   بیٹہی ہین ہم تہیه طوفان کئی ہوئے

(New Ghazal)

١٠ دیکہتا ہون وحشت شوق خروش آماده سے
خال رسوائی سرشك سر بصحرا داده سے

Ghalib 1969, p. 100.

Notes

The forms ى and ے are interchangeable: compare ہوئۓ in lines 8 and 9, and سے in lines 5 and 9. In some instances of کئی the tooth (shusha) is present but the hamza is lacking. We have normalized the spelling of ہوئی at the end of each line because it is not always clear exactly what has been written.

The retroflex consonants ڑ and ڈ are written with a small ط (ڈ inconsistently), but ٹ is written with a combination of two superscript dots and a small ط.

Line by line:

3: the three dots of the چ of چاہتا are blurred into one. The ب of دلفریبی lacks its dot, and there is an unexplained dot above the ى.

4: the verb ڈھونڈھنا is written with an initial د instead of ڈ; see also line 7. رخ په are run together.

5: مقابل میں are run together. The ش of دشنہ is written with two dots and a small stroke above it. The triangle of three dots over the ژ of مژگاں points down and is located so high that it interferes with the diagonal of کئی.

6: the 3rd dot of the پ of پہر touches the ن of دن immediately below it in line 7.

7: کہ رات دن are stacked above فرصت. The ٹ of بیٹھے is written with two dots as well as a retroflex marker.

8: دل میں are run together.

9: نہ چھیڑ are run together. The three dots of the س of جوش are written as a slanting stroke: see also شوق in line 1 of the following ghazal.

اللہ

زبدة الاماثل والاقران چودھری طالب علی صاحب تعلقدار دین پناہ زاد لطفہ

بعد نیاز آنکہ آپ کا عنایت نامہ مورخہ ۴ اپریل سنہ ۹۳ء موصول ہوا
جسمین آپ نے اپنے لڑکے محمد منظور کا نام رجسٹر امیدواران مین قایم
رہنے کی سفارش فرمائی تھی بجواب اوسکے نہایت افسوس کے ساتھ
ملتمس ہوں کہ گورنمنٹ کے احکام نسبت امیدواران کے یہہ ہین کہ تا وقتیکہ
وہ مڈل کلاس نہ پاس کرین اونکا نام درج رجسٹر امیدواران نہ کیا جاوے
لہذا نیازمند آپ کی خواہش پورا کرنے مین معذور ہے فقط زیادہ نیاز

راقم [illegible]

ڈپٹی کمشنر ضلع بارہ بنکی
۵ اپریل ۹۳

7/4/93 [illegible]

انه
زبدة الاماثل و الاقران چودهري طالب علي صاحب تعلقدار دين پناه زاد لطفهٗ
بعد نياز آنكه - آپ كا عنايت نامه مورخه ٤ ،اپريل سنه ١٨٩٣ ع موصول ہوا
جسمين آپ ني اپني لڑكي محمد منظور كا نام رجسٹر اميدواران مين قايم
رهني كي سفارش فرمائ تهي - بجواب اوسكي نہايت افسوس كي ساتہه
ملتمس ہون كه گورنمنٹ كي احكام نسبت اميدواران كي يہه ہين كه تا وقتيكه
وه مڈل كلاس نه پاس كرين اونكا نام درج رجسٹر اميدواران نه كيا جاوي
لہذا نيازمند آپ كي خواهش پورا كرني مين معذور هي فقط زياده نياز -
راقم
ڈپٹي كمشنر ضلع باره بنكی
٥ ،اپريل ٩٣

A letter from the Deputy Commissioner, Bara Banki (U.P.) to a local landholder. From a private collection.

Notes

Aspirated consonants are indicated by both forms of ه: compare چودهرى in line 2 with تهى in line 5. A small ھ is used as a subscript diacritic with the various forms of ہ. Only ى with two subscript dots is used in final position.

Line by line:

3: the small stroke between ٤ and اپريل, represented in the transcription by a comma, was used to mark the day of the month in dates; see also line 11 and Guide no. 12. For the truncated ع above the end of ١٨٩٣, see Guide IV.

5: the aspirated ت of ساتہه is indicated by writing ہ twice: see also يہه in line 6 and Exx. 6:9, 49:4, 64:4, 65:3.

9: the ق of راقم is extended in a decorative flourish, which in turn has caused the writer to use an alternate form of ک in کمشنر below it in line 10.

لزوم سی حرم کو محترم کیا صلی اللہ علیہ وآلہ وسلم وشرف وکرم **ذکر مبارک حضرت محمد صلی اللہ
علیہ وآلہ وسلم کی دودہ پلانیکا اور حلیمہ رضی اللہ عنہا کی دائی ہونیکا** عرب مین دستور
تہا کہ ہر برس مین دو بار عورتین شیر دار مکی مین آنکر لڑکونکو لیکر اپنی مکانونکو جاتی تہین جب مدت دودہ پلانیکی
پوری ہوتی تہی تو مکی مین لڑکونکو باپ مان کی پاس پہونچاکر انعام اکرام لیکر اپنی مکانونکو جاتی تہین اتفاقاً اوس
برس مین بنی سعد کی قبیلہ کی عورتین مکی مین آئین اونمین حلیمہ سعدیہ ابو ذویب کا قبیلہ آیا اور اوس سال اونکی
ملک مین قحط تہا حلیمہ رضہ اور اوسکا خاوند ایک دبلی سی گدہی پر اور ضعیف سی اونٹنی پر سوار ہوکر چلی تہی بڑی
مصیبت سے مکی مین پہونچی قافلی کی عورتون نے آگی سی پہونچکر مقدور والون کی بچی لی لیے اور محمد بن عبد اللہ کی لینے کا
کوئی ارادہ نکرتی تہی اسواسطی کہ وہ یتیم تہی اور انعام دائیونکا باپ سی تعلق رکہتا تہا حلیمہ نے اپنی خاوند سی
کہا کہ مین تو خالی وطن کو نجاونگی اگر تیری صلاح ہو تو ابو طالب کی یتیم کو کہ جسکی پیشانی سی نور اور برکت چمکتا ہی
لیچلین وہ خاوند کو راضی کرکے آمنہ کی پاس گئی اور اونکی زبانی وہ کرامتین اور خوبیان جو حمل اور تولد مین دیکہی
تہین سنکر بڑی خوشی سی لیکر خاوند کی پاس آئی اور احوال جو آمنہ سی سنا تہا سنایا ابو ذویب خوش ہوا اور

١ لزوم سے حرم کو محترم کیا صلی اللہ علیه و آله و سلم و شرف و کرم ذکر مبارک
حضرت محمد صلی الله

٢ علیه و آله و سلم کی دوده پلانیکا اور حلیمه رضی الله عنہا کے دائی ہو نیکا عرب مین
دستور

٣ تہا که ہر برس مین دو بار عورتین شیردار مکے مین آنکر لڑکونکو لیکر اپنے مکانونکو
جاتی تہین جب مدت دوده پلانیکی

٤ پوری ہوتی تہی تو مکے مین لڑکونکو باپ مان کے پاس پونہچا کر انعام اکرام لیکر
اپنے مکانونکو جاتی تہین اتفاقاً اوس

٥ برس مین بنی سعد کے قبیله کی عورتین مکے مین آئین اونمین حلیمه سعدیه ابو
ذویب کا قبیله آیا اور اوس سال اونکے

٦ ملك مین قحط تہا حلیمه اور اوسکا خاوند ایك دبلے سے گدہے پر اور ضعیف سی
اونٹنی پر سوار ہو کر چلے تہے بڑی

٧ مصیبت سے مکے مین پونہچے قافلے کی عورتون نے آگے سے پونہچکر مقدور والون
کے بچے لے لیے اور محمد بن عبدالله کے لینے کا

٨ کوئی اراده نکرتی تہی اسواسطے که وه یتیم تہے اور انعام دائیونکا باپ سے تعلق
رکہتا تہا حلیمه نے اپنے خاوند سے

٩ کہا که مین تو خالی وطن کو نجاؤنگی اگر تیری صلاح ہو تو ابو طالب کے یتیم کو که
جسکی پیشانی سے نور اور برکت چمکتا ہے

١٠ لیچلین وه خاوند کو راضی کر کے آمنه کے پاس گئی اور اونکی زبانی وه کرامتین اور
خوبیان جو حمل اور تولد مین دیکہین

١١ تہین سُنکر بڑی خوشی سے لیکر خاوند کے پاس آئی اور احوال جو آمنه سے سُنا تہا
سُنایا ابو ذویب خوش ہوا اور

Muhammad Tahir 1289, p. 102.

Notes

A truncated ی is generally used to render ے. For the symbols following the names of the Prophet Muhammad, his mother, Amina, and his wet-nurse Halima, see Guide II.

Line by line:

4: the verbs پہنچنا and پہنچانا are spelled ... پونہچ; see also line 7.

11: there is a conventional mark above اور to signal a change of topic.

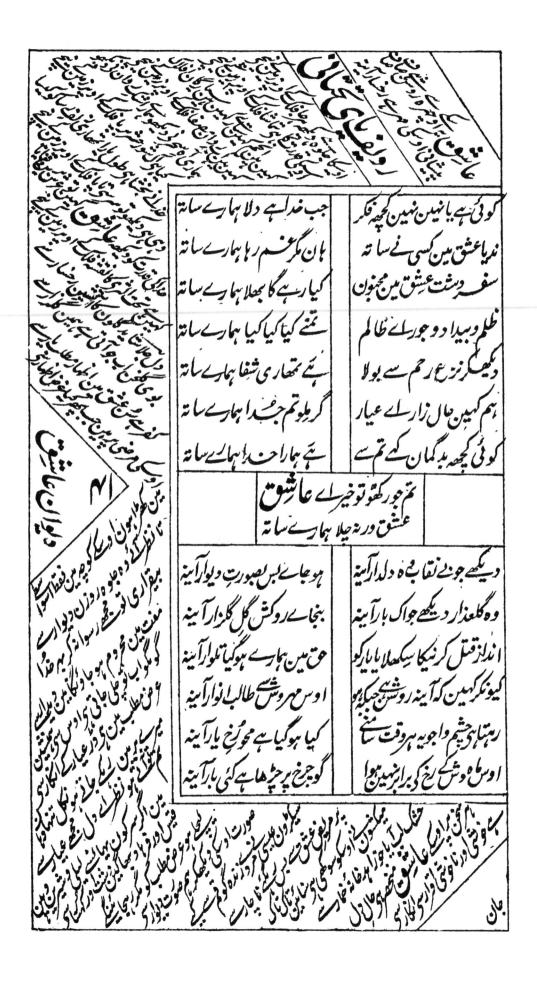

ردیف یای تحتانی

کوئی ہے یا نہین نہین کچھہ فکر | جب خدا ہے دلا ہمارے ساتہ
ندیا عشق مین کسی نے ساتہ | ہان مگر غم رہا ہمارے ساتہ
سفر دشت عشق مین مجنون | کیا رہے گا بھلا ہمارے ساتہ
ظلم و بیداد و جور اے ظالم | تمنے کیا کیا کیا ہمارے ساتہ
دیکھکر نزع رحم سے بولا | ہے تمھاری شفا ہمارے ساتہ
ہم کہین حال زار اے عیار | گر ملو تم جدا ہمارے ساتہ
کوئی کچھہ بدگمان کہے تم سے | ہے ہمارا خدا ہمارے ساتہ

تم جو رکھو تو خیر اے عاشق
عشق ورنہ چلا ہمارے ساتہ

دیکھے جو بے نقاب وہ دلدار آئینہ | ہو جائے بس بصورت دیوار آئینہ
وہ گلعذار دیکھے جو اک بار آئینہ | بنجائے روکش گل گلزار آئینہ
انداز قتل کرنیکا سکھلایا یار کو | حق مین ہمارے ہوگیا تلوار آئینہ
کیونکر کہین کہ آئینہ روشن ہے جبکہ ہو | اوس مہروش سے طالب انوار آئینہ
رہتا ہی چشم وا جو یہ ہر وقت سامنے | کیا ہوگیا ہے محو رخ یار آئینہ
اوس ماہ وش کے رخ کی برابر نہین ہوا | گو چرخ پر چڑھا ہے کئی بار آئینہ

جان

The first ghazal transcribed begins in the upper margin immediately below the words **ردیف یای تحتانی**. The second ghazal begins with a conventional mark over the first two words: **دل جلا**, and continues to the lower right corner.

١ اوسیکا جلوہ ہے دیکھہ ہر جا فلک کے اوپر زمین کے نیچے
اوسیکی قدرت کا ہی تماشا فلک کے اوپر زمین کے نیچے
٢ کہین ہین انجم کہین ستارے کہین ہین سیارگان افلاک
کہین ہین آبِ روان مصفا فلک کے اوپر زمین کے نیچے
٣ ہماری آہِ سحر نے دیکھو ہمارے اشکِ رواں نے دیکھو
کیا ہی اک شور حشر برپا فلک کے اوپر زمین کے نیچے
٤ خدا نے بخشا ہی طول یارا تمھاری زلفِ رسا کو کیسا
وہی ہے دیکھو تو سر سے تا پا فلک کے اوپر زمین کے نیچے
٥ خدا کی قدرت کو دیکھہ عاشِق کہین تو عرش برین بنایا
کہین ہے تحت الثرے کا نقشہ فلک کے اوپر زمین کے نیچے

٦ دل جلا شاید گلون کا آتشینِ رخسار سے
بوی گلخن اب جو آتی ہے ہمین گلزار سے
٧ کفر ہے سُن عشق مین اظہار مطلب یار سے
اوسکی مرضی پر ہین جب پھر کیا غرض اظہار سے
٨ مین کھڑا ہون اوسکے کوچہ مین فقط اسواسطے
تا نظر آئے وہ جلوہ روزن دیوار سے
٩ بیقراری تو مجھے رسوا نہ کر بہر خدا
مفت مین محروم ہو جاؤنگا مین دیدار سے
١٠ گو مگو اب تو چلی جاتی ہے اوس سے ہمنشین
عرض مطلب مین ہے ڈر عیار کے انکار سے
١١ میرے بر مین رہکے جاتے ہو نکل تنہا وہان
تم تو آتے ہو نظر اے دل مجھے عیار سے
١٢ مین اگر سر کون یہانسے لیلی و شیرین وہین
قیس اور فرہاد و بھاگین دشت اور کہسار سے

قیس اور فرہاد و بھاگین دشت اور کہسار سے

١٣ لیچلے ہو عرض مطلب کو مگر رہجائینگے

صورت اوسکی دیکھکر ہم صورت دیوار سے

١٤ سیکڑون عیسی نے مردے زِندہ گو قم سے کیے

پر مریضِ عشق سے بس رہگئے نا چار سے

١٥ میکشون نے اوسکو سوکھی ہے نسائین تاک تاک

خشك لب آیا جو زاہد خانۂ خمار سے

١٦ ہر سخن پر اوسکے عاشِق منحصر ہے حالِ دل

ہے خوشی اور ناخوشی اقرار سے انکار سے

١٧ جان

‘Ashiq 1879, p. 41.

Notes

The last word in the lower right corner, جان, is a tark indicating the first word of the next page; see also Ex. 65:9. The two ghazals in the box in the center of the page are not transcribed. A truncated ی is often used to represent ے. The writing in the margin is an example of کھپانا, "to pack in a small space."

Line by line:

1: ہے is written above جلوه, with its hook below the د of دیکھ. کے is written above the preceding word, and likewise throughout in the *radif*.

4: the ف of زلف touches the ر of رسا.

5: the بر of برین is written above the ش of عرش, displacing its dots to the right.

حضرت ولی نعمت آیۂ رحمت سلامت

بعد تسلیم معروض ہے حق تعالیٰ جل جلالہ و عم نوالہ جس گروہ پر مہربان ہوتا ہے وہاں حاکم
عادل رحیم بھیجتا ہے کہ وہ بقوت عاملہ کفر و بدعت کی جڑ اوکھاڑ ڈالے اور بصفت رحم رعایا
کو پالے مصداق اسکا ذات قدسی صفات جناب عالی ہے ہر قمار خانے کی بنا مٹا ڈالی ہے زہی نوکر
سپاہ غلہ کا محصول معاف کر دیا ہے روپیہ عیشت پر نثار کیا ہے زہی آئین ریاست

[illegible]

پیر و مرشد حضرت فردوس مکان کا دستور تھا کہ جب میں قصیدہ بھیجتا تھا
اوسکی رسید میں خط تحسین و آفرین کا شرماتا ہی کہتی ہوئے مگر اپنی بغیر بنتی نہیں
کہ ہندوی او سخط میں ملفوف عطا ہوا کرتے تھے اور قصیدہ مدحیہ میرے دیوان فارسی میں کہ قوم
اور وہ دیوان حضرت کے کتابخانے میں موجود ہے خطوط کے تصدیق از روئے دفتر ہو سکتی ہے
یہ رسم جاری نہیں ہے اگر جاری رہے تو بہتر ہے زیادہ حد ادب التفات کا طالب غالب

[illegible]

۱ حضرت ولی نعمت آیۀ حمت سلامت

۲ بعد تسلیم معروض ہی حق تعالے جلّ جلاله و عم نواله جس گروه پر مهربان ہوتا
ہی وہان حاکم

۳ عادل رحیم بہیجتا ہی که وه بقوّت عادله کفر و بدعت کی جڑ اوکہاڑ ڈالی اور بصفت
رحم رعایا

٤ کو پالی مصداق اسکا ذات قدسے صفات جناب عالی ہی که قمار خانیکی بنا مٹا ڈالی
ہے زہی قانون

۵ سیاست غلّه کا محصول معاف کر دیا ہی روپیه رعیّت پر نثار کیا ہی زہی آئین ریاست
(بیت)

رباعی
نوّاب که شد ز شوکت اقبالش
بخشیدن باج غلّه از اقبالش
فارغ شد ہرکتی در داد فراغ
ہم فارغ و ہم فراغ باشد سالش ۱۲۸۱

٦ پیر و مرشد حضرت فردوس مکان کا دستور تہا که جب مین قصیده بہیجتا

۷ اوسکی رسید مین خط تحسین و آفرین کا شرم آتی ہی کہتی ہوئے مگر
کہی بغیر بنتی نہین ۲۵۰

۸ کے ہنڈوی اوسخط مین طفوف عطا ہُوا کرتے تہی دو قصیدۀ مدحیّه
میرے دیوان فارسے مین مرقوم

۹ اور وه دیوان حضرت کے کتابخانیمین موجود ہے خطونکے تصدیق از
روے دفتر ہو سکتی

۱۰ یه رسم بُری نہین ہے اگر جارے رہی تو بہتر ہے زیاده حد ادب التفات کا
طالب غالب ۱۲

۱۱ (vertically in the left margin) پنجشنبه ۱۹ محرم سنه ۱۲۸۲

Chandar 1966, (unpaginated).

Notes

In final position, ی varies freely with ے. The quatrain written zig-zag in the middle of the page is in Persian. The date 1281 at the end of the quatrain indicates that the last line contains a chronogram (the abjad value of both فارغ and فراغ is 1281).

Line by line:

1: the ر of رحمت is missing from the manuscript.

2: in مہربان, the ر connects with the following با, one of the many instances of shekasta forms in this example. See Guide no. 43.

3: the retroflex marker for the ڈ of ڈالی is four dots.

4: کہ is written in the shekasta form: see also line 6. The retroflex marker for the ٹ in مٹا is four dots. The final ن of قانون is a straight diagonal.

5: following the word ریاست is a conventional symbol for بیت which signals the beginning of a verse. We have added the word بیت.

6: the conventional mark over پیر و مرشد signals a new topic.

7: the line over شرم is unexplained. 250 is written in siyaq.

8: دو is written in the shekasta form.

9: کتابخانے میں, and خطوں کے are each run together, with the keshida of the ک in the latter extended to the left. At the end of the line there are some marks that one of our readers suggests reading as ہے.

10: the numeral ۱۲ signifies "end," 12 being the abjad value of حدّ: see Guide II and Ex. 4.

غزل کا نیا منظر نامہ

شمس الرحمٰن فاروقی

گذشتہ چالیس برسوں میں نئی غزل پر دو نسلیں گذر چکی ہیں اور اب تیسری نسل ہمارے سامنے ہے۔ سوال یہ ہے کہ ان چالیس برسوں میں غزل نے کیا کھویا اور کیا پایا؟ پہلی نسل جن ناموں سے عبارت ہے ان میں بعض حسب ذیل ہیں: ناصر کاظمی، ابن انشا، سلیم احمد، خلیل الرحمٰن اعظمی، منیر نیازی، بمل کرشن اشک، عزیز حامد مدنی، جمیل الدین عالی، محبوب خزاں، باقر مہدی، حسن نعیم۔ دوسری نسل کے جو نام فوری طور پر ذہن میں آتے ہیں وہ حسب ذیل ہیں: محمد علوی، احمد مشتاق، ظفر اقبال، شہریار، کمار پاشی، فضیل جعفری، بانی، زیب غوری، شکیب جلالی، ندا فاضلی، پرکاش فکری، ساقی فاروقی، عادل منصوری۔ بعض کہتے ہیں کہ ابھی دوسری نسل کا دور دورہ ہے، اور تیسری نسل ابھی اپنی شناخت متعین نہیں کر سکی ہے۔ بعض لوگوں کا خیال ہے کہ دوسری نسل والوں کا تخلیقی جوہر اب کملا گیا ہے۔ پہلی نسل کے بہت سے لوگ تو ہمارے درمیان ہی نہیں ہیں، اور جو ہیں وہ اب زوال پا چکے ہیں۔ ان سے کوئی شکایت نہیں۔ لیکن دوسری نسل والوں سے شکوہ ہے کہ وہ اس قدر جلد بوڑھے کیوں ہو گئے؟ اگرچہ دوسری نسل والوں میں سے بھی تین کو موت نے ہم سے لے لیا، لیکن جو ہم میں موجود ہیں ان کو کیا ہو گیا ہے؟ کچھ لوگ یہ بھی کہتے ہیں کہ دوسری نسل بھی ختم تو ہو گئی، لیکن تیسری ابھی پیدا نہیں ہوئی ہے۔ لہٰذا ان لوگوں کے نزدیک ہماری غزل پر اس وقت وہی جمود و سکوت طاری ہے جو پہلی نسل کے سرگرم کار ہونے کے پہلے تھا۔

١ غزل کا نیا منظر نامه
٢ شمس الرحمن فاروقی
٣ گذشته چالیس برسوں میں نئی غزل پر دو نسلیں گذر چکی ہیں اور اب تیسری نسل
ہمارے
٤ سامنے ہے . سوال یه ہے که ان چالیس برسوں میں غزل نے کیا کھویا اور کیا پایا؟
پہلی نسل جن ناموں سے
٥ عبارت ہے ان میں بعض حسب ذیل ہیں : ناصر کاظمی ، ابن انشا ، سلیم احمد ، خلیل
الرحمٰن اعظمی ، منیر نیازی ، بمل کرشك
٦ اشك ، عزیز حامد مدنی ، جمیل الدین عالی ، محبوب خزاں ، باقر مہدی ، حسن نعیم .
دوسری نسل کے جو نام فوری طور پر ذہن میں آتے
٧ ہیں وہ حسب ذیل ہیں : محمد علوی ، احمد مشتاق ، ظفر اقبال ، شہریار ، کمار پاشی ،
فضیل جعفری ، بانی ، زیب غوری ، شکیب جلالی ،
٨ ندا فاضلی ، پرکاش فکری ، ساقی فاروقی ، عادل منصوری . بعض کہتے ہیں که ابھی
دوسری ہی نسل کا دور دورہ ہے . اور تیسری نسل ابھی اپنی شناخت
٩ متعین نہیں کر سکی ہے . بعض لوگوں کا خیال ہے که دوسری نسل والوں کا تخلیقی
جوہر اب کجلا گیا ہے . پہلی نسل کے بہت سے لوگ تو
١٠ ہمارے درمیان ہی نہیں ہیں ، اور جو ہیں ، وہ اب زوال پا چکے ہیں . ان سے کوئی
شکایت نہیں . لیکن دوسری نسل والوں سے شکوہ ہے
١١ که وہ اس قدر جلد بوڑھے کیوں ہو گئے؟ اگرچه دوسری نسل والوں میں سے بھی تین
کو موت نے ہم سے لے لیا . لیکن جو ہم میں
١٢ موجود ہیں ان کو کیا ہو گیا ہے؟ کچھ لوگ یه بھی کہتے ہیں که دوسری نسل بھی ختم
تو ہو گئی ، لیکن تیسری ابھی پیدا نہیں ہوئی ہے . لہٰذا
١٣ ان لوگوں کے نزدیك ہماری غزل پر اس وقت وہی جمود و سکوت طاری ہے جو پہلی
نسل کے سرگرم کار ہونے کے پہلے تھا .

Shamsur Rahman Faruqi, from author's autograph manuscript of a radio address delivered in Lucknow, December 25, 1990. From a private collection.

Notes

Minimization is a prominent feature of this hand. A medial tooth is often omitted, especially in common words such as نہیں, میں, and ہیں. The location of the tooth is shown by a slight elongation of the connecting line. The shape بر (as in برسوں in lines 3, 4) is recurved.

Line by line:

3: the ی of چالیس has an extra tooth.

4: the dot of the initial ن of ناموں touches the top of the following ا.

5: کرشک is a slip of the pen for کرشن, possibly influenced by the pen name اشک.

8: the ص of منصوری lacks its tooth. The خ of شناخت is minimized and suggests a ف.

9: the letters نہی of نہیں are minimized.

12: there is no tooth for the ت of ختم.

13: the ر before ہونے is an error.

4 As.

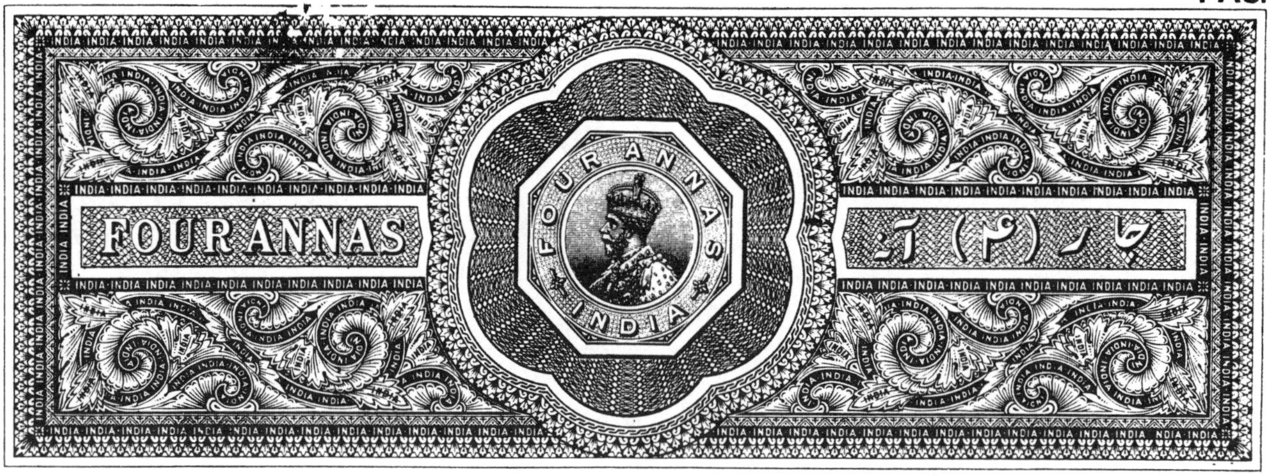

चार आना

منکہ وزیر علی ولد نواب علی قوم سید شیعہ رکابدار پورہ ساکن کوچہ میر جان شہر لکھنؤ کا ہوں

جو کہ مبلغ بتیس روپیہ کہ نصف جس کے اٹھارہ روپیہ آٹھ آنہ ہوتے ہیں سیکڑہ منافع بحساب فی صدی

آٹھ آنہ ماہواری بمدت تین سال بضرورت خود از نقد زر روپیہ مسماۃ قدسیہ سلطان بیگم صاحبہ ازان

مذکورہ بنت امجد جان بعرف بنن صاحب زوجہ نواب سید بندہ حسن صاحب [illegible]

ساکنہ حال [illegible] لکھنؤ سے قرض لیکر کل روپیہ [illegible] بقیہ زر روپیہ

معہ دیگر اقرار کرتا ہوں کہ کل روپیہ دائنہ کو قسط بندی ایک روپیہ ماہواری معہ سود منافع [illegible]

کروں گا اگر قسط مقررہ [illegible] مہینہ میں نہ ادا ہو تو دائنہ مذکورہ کو اختیار ہے

کہ کل روپیہ اصل معہ منافع [illegible] بذریعہ عدالت [illegible] جائداد منقولہ

غیر منقولہ [illegible] وصول کر لیوے لہذا یہ تمسک لکھدیا

کہ سند رہے اور وقت ضرورت کام آوے فقط

سطر ۱۲ میں [illegible] قلمزد ہیں

وزیر علی بقلم خود

المرقوم ۲۹ اگست ۱۹۳۵ء بقلم سید [illegible] علی

۷۸٦

١ منکه وزیر علی ولد نواب علی قوم سید پیشه رکابداری ساکن کوچه مرجان شہر
لکھنؤ کا ہون -

٢ جو که مبلغ سینتیس روپیه که نصف جسکے اٹھاره روپیه ١٨ آٹھه آنه ہوتے ہین بتقرر
منافع بحساب فیصدی

٣ آٹھه ١٨- آنه ماہواری بمدت تین سال بضرورت ادائے بقیه زر کرایه مسماۃ ذکیه
سلطان بیگم صاحبه ازان

٤ مذکوره بنت اصغر جان عرف نبن صاحب زوجه نواب سید بنده حسین صاحب انریری
مجسٹریٹ

٥ ساکنه حال نیاگاؤں شہر لکھنؤ سے قرض لیکر کل رُوپیه دائنه کو اونکے بقیه زر
کرایه مین

٦ مجرا دیکر اقرار کرتا ہون که کل روپیه دائنه کو به قسط بندی ایکروپیه ماہواری
علاوه منافع کے ادا

٧ کر دونگا اگر قسط مقرره مجهسے کسے مہینه مین ناغه ہو جاوی تو دائنه مذکوره کو
اختیار ھے

٨ که کل روپیه اپنا اصل معه منافع معه خرچه بذریعه عدالت مجهسے و میری ہر قسم
کی جائداد منقوله و

٩ غیر منقوله و ذات خاص میریسے جسطرح چاہین وصول کر لیوین لہذا یهه تمسك
لکهدیا

١٠ که سند رهے اور وقت ضرورت کے کام آوی فقط

١١ سطر ٤ میں (ساکنه) قلمزد ہے -

١٢ العبد وزیر علی بقلم خود

١٣ المرقوم ٢٩ ،اگست سنه ١٩٣٥ ع بقلم سید شوکت علی

Right hand margin:

١٤ العبد وزیر علی بقلم خود

١٥ گواه شد عبد الحئی (؟) بقلم خود

١٦ گواه شد مرزا علی امجد بقلم خود

A promissory note, from a private collection. The document was executed on official "stamped" paper, showing the profile of King George V.

Notes:

The two forms of ی are distinguished. Aspirated consonants are consistently indicated by ه: see, e.g., the لکهنؤ in lines 1 and 5 and اٹهاره and آٹهه in line 2. The signatures of the borrower and two witnesses are arranged at right angles to the text along the right margin. Original reduced 10%.

Line by line:

Top of the page: the number 786 is the abjad equivalent of بسم الله الرحمٰن الرحیم. See Guide IV.

2: the amount thirty-seven rupees is indicated in words as well as in siyaq forms, while the amount eighteen rupees is shown in words, numerals, and siyaq forms. The amount in annas is indicated in words only; the numerals and siyaq forms are written above the relevant words.

3: the numeral ۱۸ appears to be an error for ۸.

4: in صاحب the ح is a continuation of the ا. See Guide no. 30. The scribe has crossed out a misplaced word, ساکنه, and has mentioned the fact at the end of the document in line 11: this change is confirmed by the signer of the note in line 12.

5: ان is written اون. The ن of مین curves back to include the dot; this form is also seen in Ex. 74, esp. lines 6, 10.

6: the amount one rupee is indicated in words with the siyaq equivalent written above.

9: the ص of خاص and the ل of وصول are extended.

10: که is written as a logograph, as is کے. For فقط, see Guide no. 8.

12: and right-hand margin: the phrase بقلم خود was the conventional way of indicating that the name was actually signed by the person and not written by someone else. The name of the first witness is difficult to decipher.

نمونہ رقعہ عند الطلب

منکہ خدا بخش ولد الٰہی بخش قوم جولاہا ساکن کٹرہ بستی خلد آباد شہر الہ آباد کا ہوں
اس تحریر کی رو سے میں اقرار کرتا ہوں کہ مبلغ بیس روپیہ جس کا نصف
دس روپیہ ہوتا ہے مسمی رام کشن ولد بنا لال بقال ساکن محلہ کٹرہ آباد شہر الہ آباد
کو عند الطلب مقام الہ آباد پر میں معہ سود بحساب فیصدی ایک سیکڑہ ماہوار
تا روز وصول ادا کر دوں گا۔ لہذا یہ چند کلمہ بطور رقعہ پرامیسری نوٹ کے لکھ دیا
کہ سند رہے اور بوقت ضرورت پر کام آوے۔ المرقوم ۱۱ اکتوبر سنہ ۱۹۱۵ع
(ٹکٹ رسید آنہ لگا کر اس پر دستخط ہوں گے۔)

العبد
دستخط بخط ہندی خدا بخش بقلم خود

١ نمونه رقعه عند الطلب

٢ منکه خدا بخش ولد اله بخش قوم جولاہا ساکن نئی بستی خلدآباد شهر اله آباد کا هوں

٣ اس تحریر کے رو سے منمقر اقرار کرتا هوں که مبلغان بیس روپیه که نصف

٤ اوس کا دس روپیه هوتا هے مسمی رام کشن ولد پنا لال بقال ساکنمحله خلدآباد شهر
اله آباد

٥ کو عند الطلب مقام اله آباد میں معه سود بحساب فیصدی ۲ سیکڑا ماهوار

٦ تا روز وصول ادا کرونگا - لهذا یهه چند کلمه بطور رقعه پرامیسری نوٹ کے لکهدیا

٧ که سند رهے اور ضرورت پر کام آوے - المرقوم ١١ ، اکتوبر سنه ١٩١٥ ع

٨ (ٹکٹ رسیدا چسپان هوکر اسپر دستخط هوگا -)

٩ العبد

١٠ دستخط بخط هندی خدا بخش بقلم خود

Siddiqui 1941, p. 118.

Notes

This book was extensively used in schools to teach students to prepare commercial and legal documents. This example is a promissory note.

Final اد as in آباد, که, final ب, and recurved final ں are worthy of note.

Line by line:

3: 20 is written in siyaq above the word بیس.

4: ساکن محله are run together. 10 is written in siyaq above the word دس.

8: رسیدی is written incorrectly as رسیدا.

14. 8-76

برادرم آداب

ادھر آپ روانہ ہوئے — دو ایک ہی دن بعد مجھے دہلی جانا پڑا —
واپس آیا تو آپ کا خط ملا کہ زبانی مبارکباد دے سکا ہوں
ہمیں خوش خبری کے سلسلے میں جو آپ نے ذریعے بھیجی تھی —
بے حد مسرت ہوئی ۔ ہم دونوں کی طرف سے دعائیں —
آپ نے گراں نامے میں ذکر کیا جس میں آپ نے ازراہ
لطف و محبت میری تعریف و توصیف بڑھا چڑھا کر
کر رکھی تھی — میری وہی تحریر جب آپ
نے سمجھی گزشتہ دنوں خود آپ نے ہم دوستوں
سے بحث کے سلسلے میں یاد دی —

اک نشانی ملفوف ہے —

والسلام
[illegible]

برادر مکرم آداب
ادھر آپ روانہ ہوئے ۔ دوسرے ہی دن مجھے دہلی جانا پڑا ۔
جامعہ بھی گیا تا کہ شمیم صاحب کو زبانی مبارکباد دے دوں
اس خوش خبری کے سلسلے میں جو آپ کے ذریعے پہنچی تھی ۔
بے حد مسرّت ہوئی کہ وہ وہاں خوش و خرّم ہیں ۔
آپ کے گرامی نامے کا بھی ذکر کیا جس میں آپ نے از راہ
لطف و محبّت میری تعریف و توصیف بڑھ چڑھ
کر انھیں لکھی تھی ۔ میں ویسا تو نہیں جیسا آپ
نے سمجھ لیا مگر یہ دعا ضرور کرتا ہوں کہ دوستوں کے
حسن ظن کے مطابق بنا دے ۔
اجازت نامہ ملفوف ہے ۔ والسلام
مخلص اکبر

A personal letter from a private collection.

Notes

In this modern example a functional distinction is made between ھ and ہ, and the hamza is not indicated. An attempt is made to distinguish between ن and ں : compare the ن of دن in line 2 and of حسن in line 10 with the ں of دوں in line 3 and of وہاں in line 5. Certain forms are highly stylized, such as آپ, صاحب, میں, and some words are written almost vertically, such as مجھے in line 2 and تھی in line 8.

Line by line:

2: ے is written three different ways in the words دوسرے ، ہوئے, and مجھے.

4: کے is written (twice) as a logograph. See also lines 6, 9, 10.

5: وہ is written as a single penstroke. The ش of خوش is recurved.

7: the last word has been corrected and overwritten.

۲۹ ع

حضرت والد نعیم ظلہم العالی — آداب — یہاں میرے کلاس فیلو فرصت کے وقت
تفریح شطرنج گنجفہ چوسر تاش کھیلا کرتے ہیں مجھے بھی اجازت ہو تو لکھئے کہ کھیلا کروں
لکھیں — ایک تفریح طبع ہے — ہم کلاس فیلو سے محبت اور اتحاد خاطر ہوتا ہے بلکہ ورزش بھی
عریضہ فرزند علی — ۲۷ اپریل سنہ ۹۰

۳۰ ع

عزیز فرزند برخوردار علی احمد سلمہ اللہ تعالیٰ — بعد از دعائے صحت و عمر واضح ہو کہ
خیریت نامہ تمہارا میری نظر سے گذرا — جس قدر نام کھیلوں کے تم نے لکھے ہیں وہ سب کھیل
قماربازوں کے ہیں کھیلنے کی چیزیں ہیں الا ایک شطرنج جس میں تفریح اور ترقی فکر
اور زیادہ دور کے متصور ہے اگر کبھی فرصت اور طبیعت کو رغبت ہو تو صرف ایک دو بازی
شطرنج کی کھیل لیا کرو ورنہ زیادہ اور ہمیشہ بری شرط ہے اور حرف تمہارا تمہارا الحکم ہے تمہیں
معلوم رہے کہ تضیع ضائع اوقات ہوتی ہے خیریت رقیمہ صبا کا علی — ۲۸ اپریل سنہ ۹۰

١ نمره ٢٩
٢ حضرت ولی نعمے دام ظلهٗ - آداب - یہان میرے کلاس فیلو فرصت کی وقت
٣ تفریحاً شطرنج گنجفه چوسر تاش کهیلا کرتے ہین مجہے بہے اجازت ہو که انکی
شریك ہوا کرون
٤ اسمین ایك تفریح طبع ہے - دوم کلاس فیلو سے محبت اور ارتباط بڑہتا ہے باقی
کورنش
٥ عریضه فرزند علے - ٢٧ اپریل سنه ٩٠

٦ نمره ٣٠
٧ عزیز فرزند برخوردار ارجمند سلمه الله تعالے - بعد از دعاے دولت و عمر واضح ہو
که
٨ خیریت نامه تمہارا میرے نظر سے گذرا - جسقدر نام کہیلون کے تمنی لکہے ہین وه
سب کہیل
٩ قماربازون کے ہت کہنڈے کے چیزین ہین الا ایك شطرنج جسمین تفریح اور ترقی فکر
١٠ اور بند و بست کے متصور ہے اگر کبہے فرصت اور طبیعت کو رغبت ہو تو صرف ایك
دو بازے
١١ شطرنج کی کہیل لیا کرو نه زیاده اور یهه بہی شرط ہے که حریف تمہارا تمہارا
ہمچشم یا تمسے
١٢ اعلی درجه کا شریف خاندان ہو باقی خیریت رقیمه مبارک علی - ٢٨ اپریل سنه ٩٠

Abu al-Hasan 1891, p. 73.

Notes

Two successive passages have been transcribed.

This book, one of many such publications, shows the shekasta as it was taught in high schools in India until the fourth decade of this century. It teaches manners and general knowledge together with the art of letter writing, in the form of instructive correspondence between fathers and sons.

The three dots of ش are indicated by a vertical stroke; see also Ex. 9:4.

Line by line:

1: the symbol written under the ۲۹ (and under the ۳۰ in line 6) means "number": see Guide no. 12.

5: the ی of عریضه is very tall.

8: the final ہ of وہ is indicated by a large circle, open to the right, but see a similar form at the end of کہنڈے in line 9, which in this case does not appear to represent ہ.

9: ہتھکنڈے is misspelled ہت کھنڈے.

11: the repetition of تمہارا is a mistake.

لوحات تاریخیه بیتلری حسام الدین‌ها کشفلری محبوبدر

تاریخی

ماشاءالله حکیم محمود نعمت الله حسنی و محبوب و محمود ترک بوگون اودی شیخ امجدی رمضاندار محبوب سنانک ترک فلیبی فن ... اولیا مسلم

تاریخی ... خوشنودلی ... اونلرینک بوشنلق اودنی خطاط خوبلی اودلری صحیح کلماتلر اودعیات مدار ...

تاریخی ... اتوش ... نعمت الله ... ۲۳ اکتوبر ۱۹۹۶ ده ... حسام الدین ... کشفلدر محبوب

١ نقل رپورٹ منشے حسام الدین صاحب تحصیلدار فتحپور

٢ جنابعالے

٣ بیان حکیم محمد فضل اللہ رئیس قصبہ فتحپور و ممبر دسترکٹ بورڈ اور شیخ امجد
حسین زمیندار فتحپور سے سائل کی نیك جلنے اور لیاقت علم فارسے و عربے کی

٤ پائی جاتے ھے عبارت جو لکھوای گئے ھے اور منسلك رپورٹ ہذا ھے اوس خط نے
خوشخط اور املا کا صحیح لکھنا ظاہر ھے - اور حساب مین مداخلت

٥ پائی جاتے ھے - رپورٹ ہٰذا تعمیلاً ارسال ھے - ٢٦ اکتوبر سنہ ٩٤ ع دستخط منشے
حسام الدین صاحب تحصیلدار فتحپور

جناب عالی

بنام حکیم محمد مظہر رحمہ نے سہیل مختار و محمد دستگیر نوابہ اور ہم رحمہ مسیح سید اسحاق ارکی

سال کی یہاں جیسی اور ایسا نثار و سے کی جائیداد تھی —

عبارت جو سمجھ لگے گی اور روپے بلا وجہ اور خوشخط اور املا صحیح لکھنا چاہیے

اور حسب مداخلت نا جائز ہے — روپیہ لکھتا رہا ہے — ۲۶ اکتوبر ۱۹۹۲

وسط سے مسلم الا حکم الملک شکریہ در

سلطان ابو الحسن

١ جنابعالے

٢ بیان حکیم محمد فضل الہ رئیس فتحپور و ممبر دسترکت بورد اور شیخ
امجد حسین زمیندار فتح پور سے

٣ سائل کی نیك چلنی اور لیاقت علم فارسے و عربے کی پائی جاتے هی -

٤ عبارت جو لکھوائی گئے هی اور منسلك رپورٹ ہٰذہ هی اوس سے خوشخط
اور املا کا صحیح لکھنا ظاهر هے

٥ اور حساب مین مداخلت پائی جاتی هے - رپورٹ ہذہ تعمیلاً ارسال هی -
٢٦ اکتوبر سنه ١٨٩٢ ع

٦ دستخط منشے حسام الدین صاحب تحصیلدار فتح پور

٧ نقل مطابق اصل

Letter from a private collection.

Notes

These two Examples are copies of a report by a *tahsildar* on the qualifications of a candidate for legal apprenticeship at the court of the Deputy Commissioner, Bara Banki (U.P.), India.

Both copies, made in the 1940s, are examples of rapidly-written shekasta. Two copies of the same note are presented here to remind the reader that even practiced copyists could misread handwriting and make mistakes.

In neither Example are ی and ے distinguished: this is most clearly evident in پائی جاتے هے in lines 4, 5, 8, and 10. Diacritical dots are only minimally supplied. Retroflex consonants are not consistently indicated.

Line by line (for text on p. [266] only):

3: کی is written twice as a logograph.

4: the words خط نے after اس are an interpolation and should have been crossed out. The word بھی after حساب میں is an error and has been crossed out.

5: the date, '94, is incorrect.

INDEX OF EXAMPLES

1	Welch 1979, pl. 1
2	Meredith 1973, pl. 12
3	Safadi 1979, pl. 113
4	Davani 1307, p. 220
5	A nowruz card
6	Stewart 1825, pl. 21
7	Stewart 1825, pl. 19
8	Stewart 1825, pl. 15
9	Stewart 1825, pl. 9/1
10	Stewart 1825, pl. 9/2
11	Stewart 1825, pl. 11
12	Stewart 1825, pl. 10
13	Stewart 1825, pl. 12
14	Stewart 1825, pl. 13/3
15	Stewart 1825, pl. 17
16	Stewart 1825, pl. 14/18
17	Stewart 1825, pl. 20/16
18	Stewart 1825, pl. 14/17
19	Stewart 1825, pl. 24
20	Stewart 1825, pl. 18
21	Stewart 1825, pl. 10
22	Stewart 1825, pl. 16
23	Stewart 1825, pl. 22
24	Stewart 1825, pl. 13/4
25	Stewart 1825, pl. 20/11
26	Vahed 1369, pp. 594
27	Vahed 1369, pp. 603
28	Vahed 1369, pp. 579
29	Vahed 1369, pp. 533
30	Vahed 1369, pp. 419
31	Safa'i 1346, p. 272
32	Safa'i 1346, p. 11
33	Safa'i 1346, p. 150
34	Safa'i 1346, p. 17-18
35	Safa'i 1346, p. 403
36	Levy 1951, p. 116
37	*Specimens* 1902, p. 155
38	*Specimens* 1902, p. 29
39	*Specimens* 1902, p. 83
40	*Specimens* 1902, p. 117
41	*Specimens* 1902, p. 143
42	*Specimens* 1902, p. 101
43	*Specimens* 1902, p. 21
44	*Specimens* 1902, p. 57
45	*Specimens* 1902, p. 99
46	*Specimens* 1902, p. 53
47	*Specimens* 1902, p. 147
48	*Specimens* 1902, p. 95
49	*Specimens* 1902, p. 139
50	*Specimens* 1902, p. 61
51	Levy 1951, p. 114
52	Levy 1951, p. 118
53	*Ganjina* 1370, p. 15
54	Private diary
55	Aini 1978, p. 42
56	Gasanli 1983, pp. 10-11
57	*Afghanistan* 1992, p. 121
58	*Afghanistan* 1993, p. 35
59	Private collection
60	Khomeyni 1369, pp. 67
61	Khomeyni 1369, pp. 167
62	Private collection
63	Private collection
64	Barker 1977, p. 164
65	Urdu manuscript
66	Ghalib 1969, p. 100
67	Private collection
68	Tahir 1289, p. 102
69	‘Ashiq 1879, p. 41
70	Chandar 1966 (unpaged)
71	Private collection
72	Private collection
73	Siddiqui 1941, p. 118
74	Private collection
75	Abu al-Hasan 1891, p. 73
76	Private collection

LIST OF SOURCES

'Ashiq, Pandit Kanhayya Lal. *Diwan.* Lucknow, 1879.

Abu al-Hasan, Maulana. *Maktubat-e hasan.* Lucknow, 1891.

Afghanistan Mirror 3 (1992), 4 (1993).

Aini, K. S. *Kniga Zhizni Sadridina Aini.* Dushanbe, 1978.

Barker, M. A. R., et al. *Classical Urdu Poetry.* Ithaca, 1977.

Chandar, Prithvi, ed. *Muraqqa'-e ghalib ma' hawashi.* New Delhi, 1966.

Davani, Jalal al-Din. *Akhlaq-e Jalali.* Lucknow, A.H. 1307.

Faza'eli, Habibollah. *Ta'lim-e khatt.* Tehran, A.I. 2536.

_____. *Atlas-e khatt.* Tehran, 1391 Š.

Ganjina-ye asnad 1 (1370 Š).

Gasanli, G. Yu. *Sbornik dlya chteniya po persidskomu yazyku.* Dushanbe, 1983.

Ghalib, Mirza Asadullah Khan. *Diwan-e ghalib nuskha-ye shirani.* Lahore, 1969.

Jones, William. *A Grammar of the Persian Language.* London, 1771.

Khomeyni, Ruhollah. *Sahifa-ye nur.* Tehran, 1369 Š.

Law, H. D. Graves. *Persian Letters: A Manual for Students of Persian.* London, 1948.

Levy, Reuben. *The Persian Language.* London, 1951.

Meredith-Owens, G.M. *Persian Illustrated Manuscripts.* London, 1973.

Ojha, Gaurishankar Hirachand. *The Palæography of India.* New Delhi, 1971.

Ouseley, William. *Persian Miscellanies: An Essay to Facilitate the Reading of Persian Manuscripts.* London, 1795.

Perry, John R. *Form and Meaning in Persian Vocabulary: The Arabic Feminine Ending.* Costa Mesa, 1991.

Richards, John R. *Document Forms for Official Orders of Appointment in the Mughal Empire.* Cambridge, 1986.

Safa'i, Ebrahim. *Asnad-e siyasi-ye dowran-e qajariya.* Tehran, 1346 Š.

Safadi, Yasin Hamid. *Islamic Calligraphy.* Boulder, 1979.

Siddiqui, Shaykh Habib Ullah. *Majmua'-e khatt-e shekast wa kaghazat-e kar-rawa'i.* Allahabad, 1941.

Specimens of Persian Manuscript for the Use of Candidates for the Degree of Honour and High Proficiency Examinations in Persian. Calcutta, 1902.

Stewart, Charles. *Original Persian Letters and Other Documents.* London, 1825.

Tahir, Muhammad. *Rowzat al-asfiya 'urf qesas al-anibya.* Kanpur, A.H. 1289.

Vahed-e Nashr-e Asnad. *Gozida-ye asnad-e siyasi-ye iran va 'osmani: dowra-ye qajariya.* Vol. 1. Tehran, 1369 Š.

Welch, Stuart Cary. *Wonders of the Age.* Cambridge MA, 1979.

BIBLIOGRAPHY

This bibliography includes works devoted wholly or in part to teaching the user how to read Persian handwriting. Included also are some works on Persian palaeography and diplomatics because they contain facsimiles of many documents with transcriptions in printed Persian and translations, and extensive bibliographies. Some of these sources also contain examples of siyaq.

Alavi, Bozorg, and Manfred Lorenz. *Lehrbuch der persischen Sprache.* Leipzig, 1967.
A grammar of modern Persian with samples of nasta'liq and shekasta.

Barker, Muhammad Abd-al-Rahman. *A Course in Urdu.* Vol. 1. Montreal, 1967.
Includes a discussion of the siyaq or raqam system and a table of forms.

Busse, Heribert. *Untersuchungen zum islamischen Kanzleiwesen, an Hand turkmenischer und safawidischer Urkunden.* Cairo, 1959.
An example of works on Middle Eastern diplomatics. In addition to a study of chancery practice and the content of 15th- to 18th-century documents, the book contains fifty-five plates reproducing various genres of documents from this period, with transcriptions in printed Persian and translations. It has an extensive bibliography on Islamic diplomatics, and is good source of material for learning to read manuscript documents.

Elwell-Sutton, L.P. *Elementary Persian Grammar.* Cambridge, 1963.
A grammar of modern Persian with appendices on nasta'liq and shekasta.

Faza'eli, Habib Allah. *Atlas-e Khatt.* Isfahan, 1391 Š.
A historical survey, with many examples, of the major styles of script of the Islamic world. Almost half the book is devoted to styles of script used mainly in Iran: ta'liq, divani, nasta'liq, shekasta. The emphasis is on calligraphers and their work. It is useful for its introduction to the history of the scripts. The reproductions are of fair to good quality.

_____. *Ta'lim-e khatt.* Tehran, A.I. 2536.
A manual demonstrating in detail, with many examples, the forms and proportions of letters and combinations in sols, naskh, nasta'liq, and shekasta. Earlier forms of these scripts are also analyzed. In addition, there are extensive discussions of pens, ink, paper, and other implements of writing, and many quotations from classical poetry and prose about scripts and writing. The information in the book is based on carefully documented secondary sources, and the author's own experience as a calligrapher.

Fekete, L. *Einführung in die persische Paläographie: 101 persische Dokumente.* Ed. by G. Hazai. Budapest, 1977.

The documents span the period from 1396 to 1701-02 and were written in the Ottoman Empire, Khorasan, and Central Asia. In the Introduction the author comments on peculiarities of the script, formulaic expressions, and chancery practice. The documents are presented in generally high quality photographic facsimiles (reduced in size), transcription in printed Persian, and translation.

_____. *Die Siyaqat-schrift in der türkischen Finanzverwaltung.* 2 vols. Budapest, 1955.
The book deals with a form of the Arabic script, in use in Turkey until about 1880, that was written without diacritical marks. It is not identical to the siyaq/siyaqat/raqam symbols in use in the Middle East and the Subcontinent, mentioned in the Introduction to the present book, which are confined to numbers.

Forbes, Duncan. *Oriental Penmanship; An Essay for Facilitating the Reading and Writing of the Ta'lik Character.* London, 1849.
Intended to be "a Sequel and Companion to my Hindustani Grammar, published in 1846" (p. iii). Includes five plates containing quatrains in Persian, and 22 plates containing an extract from a prose narrative in Urdu. The handwriting is generally clear and easy. There are no examples of shekasta. (There are also fourteen transcriptions of plates from the author's *Hindustani Grammar*).

Karimi, Asghar. "'Hesab-e siyaq' ya 'hesab-e dinari.'" *Mardom shenasi va farhang-e 'amma-ye iran* 3 (A.I. 2536):91-100.

_____. "Vahed-ha-ye andaza-giri dar il-e bakhtiyari va hesab-e siyaq." *Mardom shenasi va farhang-e 'amma-ye iran* 1 (1353 Š):47-57.

Kazem Zadeh, H. "Les Chiffres siyâk et la comptabilité persane." *Revue du monde musulman* 30 (1915):1-51.

Law, H.D. Graves. *Persian Letters: A Manual for Students of Persian.* London, 1948.
A collection of fifty Persian letters, intended to "encourage and facilitate the study of Persian letters and the art ... of letter writing in Persia." Includes a list of shekasta forms, facsimiles of the letters with transcriptions in printed Persian and translations, and a vocabulary. The facsimiles are of only adequate quality.

Litten, Wilhelm. *Einführung in die persische Diplomatensprache.* 2 vols. Berlin, 1919.
A handbook for the training of translators or dragomans for the German embassy in Tehran. Vol. 2 includes 54 facsimiles of diplomatic correspondence from the period 1892-1911, with transcriptions in Latin script and translations into German. The letters provide good examples of the everyday nasta'liq and shekasta of the time.

Ouseley, William. *Persian Miscellanies: An Essay to Facilitate the Reading of Persian Manuscripts.* London, 1795.
Designed for the learner of Persian and for individuals who would serve in India.

Ouseley views nasta'liq as the key to learning shekasta. The book includes four plates of combinations and ligatures of letters and five plates of text, none of which appears to be in the hand of a native writer.

Palmer, E.H. *Oriental Penmanship. Specimens of Persian Handwriting.* London, 1886.
Intended primarily for persons planning to work in India. Includes a section on reed pens and other necessities for writing, basic letter-forms and combinations, an analysis of the forms used in writing shekasta, some examples of short documents written in shekasta with transcriptions in printed Persian and Latin script, an explanation of raqam with a table of forms, and a section on writing Devanagari script. Some of the examples of shekasta writing are identical to examples in Stewart's *Original Persian Letters* (see below).

Paper, Herbert H., and Mohammad Ali Jazayery. *The Writing System of Modern Persian.* Washington, D.C., 1955.
Contains a section which describes the major differences between a typical style of modern Persian handwriting and printed forms. While it does not describe nasta'liq and shekasta in particular, it systematically points out handwriting conventions, many of which are common in almost all styles of writing.

Ryechman, Jan, and Ananiasz Zajączkowski. *Handbook of Ottoman-Turkish Diplomatics.* The Hague, 1968.
A detailed introduction to the subject, with extensive bibliographies and many illustrations.

Smirnova, S. D., ed. *Sbornik Obraztsov Persidskikh Skoropisnykh Dokumentov.* Moscow, 1948.
A collection of facsimiles of 100 documents written in nasta'liq and shekasta, intended as a textbook for the Military Institute of Foreign Languages. Ten documents are dated A.H. 1279/1862-63 and the remainder were written between 1310 and 1320/1892 and 1902-03. Each example is accompanied by brief annotations and the 10 examples from 1279 are transcribed in typewritten Persian. Included also is a section giving 31 samples of proper Persian style for writing letters on various topics.

Specimens of Persian Manuscript for the Use of Candidates for the Degree of Honour and High Proficiency Examinations in Persian. Calcutta, 1902.
A collection of facsimiles of letters and documents from Iran and India, dating from the late 19th century to the early 20th century, published by the Board of Examiners, Fort William, under the authority of the Government of India. There are no transcriptions, and the documents are not identified. Each document has a facing blank pageon which the student could attempt to imitate the Persian script.

St. Clair-Tisdall, W. *Modern Persian Conversation-Grammar, with Reading Lessons ... and Persian Letters.* 3rd Edition. Heidelberg, 1923.